SIR HALLEY STEWART TRUST: LECTURES

I0127900

Volume 7

THE ATOMIC AGE

THE ATOMIC AGE

M. L. OLIPHANT,
P. M. S. BLACKETT,
R. F. HARROD,
BERTRAND RUSSELL,
LIONEL CURTIS
AND D. W. BROGAN

Routledge
Taylor & Francis Group

LONDON AND NEW YORK

First published in 1949 by George Allen & Unwin Ltd.

This edition first published in 2025
by Routledge
4 Park Square, Milton Park, Abingdon, Oxon OX14 4RN

and by Routledge
605 Third Avenue, New York, NY 10158

Routledge is an imprint of the Taylor & Francis Group, an informa business

British Library Cataloguing in Publication Data
A catalogue record for this book is available from the British Library

ISBN: 978-1-032-88942-9 (Set)
ISBN: 978-1-032-88112-6 (Volume 7) (hbk)
ISBN: 978-1-032-88160-7 (Volume 7) (pbk)
ISBN: 978-1-003-53644-4 (Volume 7) (ebk)

DOI: 10.4324/9781003536444

Publisher's Note
The publisher has gone to great lengths to ensure the quality of this reprint but points out that some imperfections in the original copies may be apparent.

Disclaimer
The publisher has made every effort to trace copyright holders and would welcome correspondence from those they have been unable to trace.

This book is a re-issue originally published in 1949. The language used and views portrayed are a reflection of its era and no offence is meant by the Publishers to any reader by this re-publication.

THE
SIR HALLEY STEWART TRUST

★

The objects of the Trust are *in general:*

To advance religion; to advance education; to relieve poverty; to promote other Charitable purposes beneficial to the community, and *in particular:*

1. To assist in the discovery of the best means by which "the mind of Christ" may be applied to extending the Kingdom of God by the prevention and removal of human misery;

2. To assist in the study of our Lord's life and teaching in their explicit and implicit application to the social relationships of man;

3. To express the mind of Christ in the realization of the Kingdom of God upon earth and in a national and a world-wide brotherhood;

For example:

For every Individual by furthering such favourable opportunities of education, service, and leisure as shall enable him or her most perfectly to develop the body, mind, and spirit:

In all Social Life, whether domestic, industrial, or national, by securing a just environment, and

In International Relationships, by fostering good will between all races, tribes, peoples, and nations so as to secure the fulfilment of the hope of "peace on earth":

4. To provide fees for a Lecture or Lectures annually and prizes for essays or other written compositions, and to pay for their publication and distribution;

5. To provide, maintain, and assist Lectures and Research work in Social, Economic, Psychological, Medical, Surgical, or Educational subjects;

6. To make grants to Libraries;

7. To assist publications exclusively connected with the objects of the Trust (not being newspapers or exclusively denominational);

8. To make grants to and co-operate with Societies, Organizations, and Persons engaged in the furtherance of Charitable objects similar to the objects of the Trust;

9. To use the foregoing and any such other method, whether of a like nature or not, as are lawful and reasonable and appropriate for the furtherance of the objects of the Trust.

The income of the Trust may not be used for dogmatic, theological, or ecclesiastical purposes other than the cult of the Science of God as manifest in man in the Son of Man in the person and teaching of our Lord, "The Word of God," Who "liveth and abideth forever."

SIR HALLEY STEWART LECTURES, 1948

THE ATOMIC AGE

By

M. L. OLIPHANT
F.R.S.

P. M. S. BLACKETT
F.R.S.

R. F. HARROD
F.B.A.

BERTRAND RUSSELL
F.R.S.

LIONEL CURTIS
M.A.

D. W. BROGAN
M.A.

———

London
GEORGE ALLEN AND UNWIN LTD

FIRST PUBLISHED IN 1949

PRINTED IN GREAT BRITAIN
in 12-*Point Caslon Type*
BY UNWIN BROTHERS LIMITED
LONDON AND WOKING

CONTENTS

I. THE SCIENTIFIC ACHIEVEMENT   *page* 11
     by M. L. Oliphant

II. MILITARY CONSEQUENCES OF ATOMIC
     ENERGY   32
     by P. M. S. Blackett

III. THE ECONOMIC CONSEQUENCES OF
     ATOMIC ENERGY   52
     by R. F. Harrod

IV. VALUES IN THE ATOMIC AGE   81
     by Bertrand Russell

V. THE POLITICAL REPERCUSSIONS OF
     ATOMIC POWER   105
     by Lionel Curtis

VI. AMERICA AS ATLAS   129
     by D. W. Brogan

I

THE SCIENTIFIC ACHIEVEMENT

M. L. OLIPHANT

In the closing years of the last century, which saw the discovery of the electron and of X-rays, the French scientist Becquerel observed that certain minerals containing uranium and thorium produced spontaneously radiations which blackened photographic plates and which caused air through which they passed to conduct electricity. From these three discoveries has grown the whole structure of modern physics and a large part of modern technology. J. J. Thomson's electron has given us radio, television, the techniques of electronics and a picture of the outer part of atoms; Röntgen's X-rays are a commonplace in medicine and tell us all we know about the arrangement of atoms in solids; Becquerel's discovery of radioactivity led directly to the release of atomic energy and to our present ideas about the structure of the core, or nucleus, of the atom. All three discoveries were the result of disinterested pursuit of the truth by men of science.

All knowledge is useful and becomes part of the cultural background of man. Scientific knowledge suffers from the disadvantage that from it spring industries which affect profoundly man's way of life, and military weapons with which man can destroy his fellows. So scientific discovery must be studied in relation to its use and misuse by mankind and no scientist can deny his own share of responsibility for the results of his labour. This direct connection between society and science means that while war is permitted and industrial supremacy is the aim of the nations, the governments of the world feel impelled to control scientific activity and dissemination of information which might be of value to an enemy. As the power of the scientist grows his freedom to follow unrestrainedly the path of knowledge is restricted. The problem of the proper relationship between science and society is increasingly acute and is the subject of other talks in this series. From the point of view of this discussion it is necessary only to remark that some important parts of the story of the release of atomic energy remain secret, though sufficient has now been freed from restriction to enable a coherent and reasonably accurate picture to be presented.

The discovery of radioactivity by Becquerel excited great interest in scientific circles, for here was a new property of matter, the spontaneous production of energy by minerals containing uranium and thorium. The Curies showed that the active substance responsible for the greater part of this radioactivity in uranium minerals was not uranium itself but was a small admixture of the rare element radium, which they were able to isolate. The activity of this concentrated material was so great that a fraction of an ounce maintained itself permanently several degrees hotter than its surroundings.

The disentangling of the complicated series of changes through which radium passes on its way to become lead was due almost entirely to Rutherford and his colleagues. Many of us have been privileged to hear the story of that work from Rutherford himself. His youthful enthusiasm in Montreal was devoted to radioactivity. Nuclear physics, which he created, remained his one real interest throughout his life. The great advances in our understanding of this complex, submicroscopic subject, which has culminated in the atomic bomb, were due to him and to that enthusiasm which he communicated to all who worked with him. It is interesting to notice that progress in this subject, which till now has been of purely academic interest, has been greater than in many branches of physics which are much more straightforward but to which no Rutherford has devoted his genius.

Rutherford and his school established that the energy changes associated with radioactive transformation were very large in comparison with the energies associated with chemical change. A pound of coal, properly burnt in a modern power-station, will produce about 1 kilowatt-hour (1 unit) of electrical energy. This chemical process of burning, in which the atoms of carbon and hydrogen in the coal combine with oxygen from the air, releases energy as heat, or motion of the molecules of the gas produced, and this disordered motion is transformed into useful power, with an efficiency approaching 30 per cent, in boilers and turbo-generators.

If a pound of radium could be made to give up its energy of transformation into lead at will, and this energy were used to heat the boilers of the power-station, it would produce more than 1 million kilo-watt-hours of electric power. Realization that changes in the nuclei of atoms were accompanied by energy emission or absorption millions of times greater than are available in chemical reactions, led at once to speculation about the possibility that this energy might one day be released for the use of mankind. Rutherford was always sceptical about this possi-bility, but success came eight years after his death.

Rutherford and Soddy showed that the radioactive change which resulted in the emission of charged particles from the nucleus produced also a change in the chemical nature of the atom—the substance was spontaneously transmuted. There followed brilliant researches by Rutherford and his collabora-tors on the scattering of α-particles by matter which were simple in concept and far-reaching in their results. Thus he initiated the modern method of nuclear research, the bombardment of elements by high-speed particles. The first fruit of this study of scattering was the formulation, with Bohr, of the nuclear model of the atom. The second was the dis-covery in 1919 of the artificial transmutation of matter—the transmutation of nitrogen into oxygen by bombardment with α-particles.

Physical scientists of the nineteenth century had

developed a picture of atoms as hard elastic balls, unchangeable by man, and were able to explain many of the properties of matter in terms of the motions of these atoms and of the attractive and repulsive forces between them. The revolutionary character of the Rutherford-Bohr picture of the atom as a sort of solar system, in which a nucleus 10,000 times smaller than the atom itself, yet containing the greater part of the mass of the atom, was surrounded by electrons, rotating in orbits like planets round the sun, lay in its substitution of emptiness for solidarity. The whole was held together by electric forces, the positive electric charge on the nucleus determining the number and arrangement of the electrons surrounding it. The interactions of the outer electrons determined the chemical properties of the atom, so that the chemical nature was determined by the nuclear charge. Thus, to change one substance into another, say lead into gold, it was necessary only to change the electric charge on the nucleus. Rutherford changed nitrogen, with seven charges on its nucleus, into oxygen, with eight, by bombarding nitrogen with α-particles, or positively charged atoms of helium, which are shot out spontaneously with very great energy, by radioactive substances like radium. The small size of the nucleus of an atom, one million-millionth of an inch in diameter, means that the chance of making a hit with an α-particle is very small, while the like electric charges on the α-particle and nitrogen nucleus repel one another, so that entry of the particle into the nucleus is difficult. Thus the efficiency of the transformation process observed by Rutherford is extremely small, only about one α-particle in a million causing a nitrogen nucleus to be transformed into an oxygen nucleus. The process is detectable only because the methods used for observing nuclear transformation are millions of times more sensitive than chemical methods available previously.

Since that time nuclear physics has followed almost as a matter of course. It was in Rutherford's laboratory that atomic transformation with artificially accelerated particles was first achieved by Cockcroft and Walton in 1932, and there, in the same year, Chadwick discovered the neutron. These two discoveries led to spectacular advances, especially because the method of artificial transmutation gave larger yields of neutrons.

The absence of electric charge rendered these new neutral particles very efficient agents with which to penetrate inside the nucleus. Fermi showed that they produced transformations in the majority of the elements similar to those produced by bombardment with charged particles such as α-particles. It was the unsatisfactory nature of Fermi's conclusions about the reactions produced in uranium which led Hahn to make a detailed study of the products by chemical methods. Hahn, at one time a pupil of Rutherford, proved that the uranium nucleus, after absorption of a neutron, sometimes underwent a complete splitting into two much simpler atoms, so discovering the unexpected phenomenon of nuclear fission.

Bohr has given a simple and satisfactory qualitative picture of what happens when a neutron invades a nucleus. With Wheeler he has developed a model based upon the fact that the interactions between particles inside the nucleus, which he regards as made up of protons and neutrons, are so strong that an incoming particle must react with them all, i.e. with the nucleus as a whole. This is in direct contrast with the action of a moving charged particle on the outer electronic structure of the atom, where, because of the loose interaction between them, individual electrons are excited to higher states, or are removed completely from the atom. In a nuclear collision which imparts energy to the struck nucleus the whole of the energy is shared among the particles, or in other words the nucleus is "heated."

These models of neutron capture can be illustrated by the differences between the behaviour of the two isotopes[1] of uranium, ^{238}U and ^{235}U.

The probability of capture by ^{238}U is vanishingly small for slow neutrons but shows a pronounced

[1] Most chemical elements consist of a mixture of two or more kinds of atoms, all possessing the same electric charge (that is containing the same number of positive particles, called "protons"), but with varying numbers of neutrons. A neutron has approximately the same mass as a proton, but has no electric charge. Hence these differing constituent atoms of a single chemical substance have masses, or weights, which are simple multiples of the mass of a proton, which is the nucleus of a hydrogen atom. Thus the masses of the separate atoms can be expressed as multiples of the mass of the hydrogen atom—e.g. the gas oxygen has two kinds of atoms, those of mass sixteen times hydrogen (^{16}O), being much more plentiful than those of mass 18 times hydrogen (^{18}O). Atoms of the same kind but different mass are called isotopes.

"resonance" at slightly higher neutron energy. We can express this in another way. A nucleus of ^{238}U will absorb readily a neutron of a certain specified energy but will ignore completely neutrons colliding with it with energies either above or below that energy, just as a violin string will "resonate" and absorb only sound waves whose frequency corresponds with its own. Capture of a neutron of mass 1 into the resonance energy band produces a nucleus of mass 239. This isotope of uranium is unstable, emitting an electron, or negatively charged particle, and transforming from uranium of nuclear electric charge (or atomic number) 92, into an element of atomic number 93, or "Neptunium." Neptunium is a chemical element unknown in the earth because it is unstable and transforms, by emission of a further electron, into element 94, or "Plutonium." We can write this in symbols:

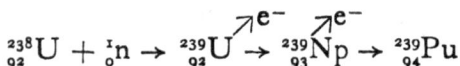

$$_{92}^{238}\text{U} + {}_0^1\text{n} \rightarrow {}_{92}^{239}\text{U} \xrightarrow{e^-} {}_{93}^{239}\text{Np} \xrightarrow{e^-} {}_{94}^{239}\text{Pu}$$

Plutonium is a comparatively stable substance. It is radioactive, emitting α-particles, or nuclei of helium atoms, and transforming into $^{235}_{92}$U, with an average lifetime for an atom of a few tens of thousands of years.

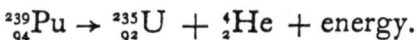

$$_{94}^{239}\text{Pu} \rightarrow {}_{92}^{235}\text{U} + {}_2^4\text{He} + \text{energy}.$$

Neptunium and Plutonium do not exist on earth because they are too short-lived to have survived and there is no natural process by which appreciable quantities can be formed in uranium.

Uranium of mass 238 also captures neutrons of very high energy. Bohr's picture of the process is then:

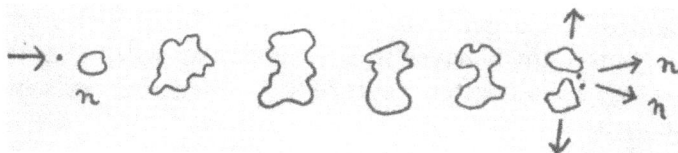

The uranium nucleus captures a neutron and becomes very "hot." The oscillations of the heated drop result in conditions which in a very short time lead to a splitting of the nucleus into two parts, the parts separating with tremendous energy. This is the phenomenon of nuclear fission, which was discovered by Hahn and verified by Meitner and Frisch. The break-up does not take place always in the same way, and the relative masses of the products vary over a wide range, with a maximum probability that the ratio of the masses is about 2 : 3.

The energy with which the fission products separate is so large that one pound of uranium undergoing fission will release as much energy as the burning of about 1,500 tons (3,760,000 lbs.) of coal. This energy is produced because the products together have a mass less than that of the original "hot" composite nucleus, the mass ΔM which disappears being transformed into kinetic energy which, according to the relationship developed by Einstein, is $W = \Delta Mc^2$, where c is the velocity of light.

Uranium of mass 235 differs from ^{238}U in that it is raised to a high enough state of excitation to undergo fission by the entry of a neutron of any energy. The probability of fission of ^{235}U for slow neutrons is large.

Plutonium behaves in a very similar way, undergoing fission after capture of a neutron of any energy.

Thorium, like ^{238}U, undergoes fission as a result of the absorption of fast neutrons only.

In all cases the products of fission are themselves radioactive, emitting one or more electrons before becoming stable elements.

This simplified picture of the fission process is not complete. There are secondary products of fission, which "evaporate" from the still "hot" fission particles. Cure-Joliot and his co-workers showed, shortly before the war, that these secondary products are neutrons, there being on the average more than two neutrons liberated per fission, the neutrons being ejected with considerable energy. This observation rendered it immediately obvious that a chain process was possible since these neutrons could cause fission in other nuclei of uranium of mass 235, though not in ^{238}U. Provided the difficulty of competitive absorption of neutrons by ^{238}U, which results in production of plutonium and not in fission, could be overcome, it was clear that there existed the possibility of power production and of an atomic bomb. The problem reduced to one of technology and of the evaluation of the exact conditions under which chain reactions actually occurred.

Suppose we imagine a mass of pure uranium metal and try to understand what would happen to the neutrons liberated in a fission process occurring near the centre of the mass. The neutrons are not fast enough on the average to initiate fission of ^{238}U. The isotope ^{235}U is present in natural uranium only to the extent of 0.7 per cent, approximately one part in 140 of the metal. Consequently the probability of collision between these neutrons and ^{235}U is much smaller than for collisions with ^{238}U. The neutrons have a long free path, that is they travel a considerable distance before they hit a nucleus, and unless the mass of metal is large they will escape from the exterior before they can produce fission in fresh ^{235}U nuclei. If the mass is very large and is extremely pure, so that the lifetime of neutrons is long because they are not captured by other substances, collisions with uranium nuclei will reduce the energy slowly. The energy lost in a single collision is very small because of the large mass difference;[1] and the neutrons will therefore loiter about for a long time in any given energy state. The probability of capture into the resonance level of ^{238}U thus becomes large. There is likely, therefore, to be too great a loss of neutrons by absorption, which does

[1] When two billiard balls of equal mass collide they can share their energy completely, but if one is much lighter than the other, very little energy is shared. Thus a tennis ball, bouncing on the ground, imparts a microscopically small part of its energy to the earth.

not lead to fission, for a chain reaction to be produced in a mass of uranium metal, however large, though this is not quite certain.

Two methods have been devised to ensure that a chain reaction will take place in a finite mass of uranium.

The first is to slow down the neutrons very rapidly by collision with some material such as heavy water[1] (deuterium) or graphite (carbon) so that when the neutrons diffuse back to the uranium the chance of resonance capture by ^{238}U is reduced, and the probability of fission of ^{235}U is greatly increased. Heavy water or graphite are used as they do not capture neutrons readily, as does ordinary water. This gives a system operating on neutrons of very low energy, and is the most obvious procedure for power production.

The second method is to concentrate the ^{235}U so that the fast fission neutrons have a proper chance to produce a chain reaction directly, or alternatively to prepare plutonium in quantity by first operating a slow neutron reacting system. Such a fast neutron chain reaction gives an extremely rapid multiplication of fissions and proceeds at a super-explosive rate —the atomic bomb.

The slow-neutron chain is best achieved with

[1] Water is mainly a combination of two hydrogen atoms of mass 1, with an oxygen atom (H_2O). However it contains also a very small trace of deuterium, which is the name given to an isotope of hydrogen of mass 2. This deuterium can be separated by an elaborate and costly process and is commonly stored as heavy water, which is water containing deuterium in place of the normal kind of hydrogen.

ordinary uranium metal by the use of graphite as a "moderator" to slow down the fission neutrons. The arrangement used is a so-called "heterogeneous pile," consisting of some tens of tons of uranium rods or slugs disposed in a calculated "lattice" throughout a mass of some hundreds of tons of graphite, which is just a dense form of carbon. Fission neutrons which escape from one of the rods, in which there is a very small chance of capture, pass into the graphite where, by multiple collisions, they lose energy rapidly. The chance that they encounter a ^{238}U nucleus before they are slowed to energies below the resonance level, is greatly reduced, and when the neutrons do diffuse to a uranium rod again they are readily captured by the ^{235}U and give rise to further fissions.

For the slow neutron chain to take place the size of the system must be greater than a very well-defined critical size, where the escape of neutrons from the surface is not greater than the rate of production. Some of the neutrons produced in fission are delayed, i.e. they are emitted only after an interval of as much as one second. This means that for a system which is only just above critical size the exponential increase in the rate of fissions, i.e. in the neutron population, takes place rather slowly. By inserting into the pile rods of a material like boron or cadmium, which absorb slow neutrons readily, the multiplication can be prevented altogether. Slow withdrawal of these rods allows the reaction to begin, and there is then plenty of time to reinsert them if the multiplication rises too rapidly. Adjustment of the rods can be carried out automatically by use of equipment like a thermostat, which sets the position of the absorbing rods so that the system runs continuously at any desired energy level.

The critical size of the system obviously depends upon the precise arrangement of the uranium and graphite and upon whether the surroundings reflect back any of the neutrons which escape from the surface. The fission energy is degenerated by collisions into heat, and the rods become hot. This heat may be extracted by cooling the rods, either by blowing gas such as air, hydrogen or helium, past them, or by surrounding them with a concentric tube through which water flows.

Unfortunately, uranium is very active chemically, and in particular it is very easily oxidized by contact with air or water. To prevent this the uranium rods or slugs must be coated with a layer of resistant metal which is in good thermal contact, but which does not absorb neutrons appreciably. There are very few metals which fulfil these conditions and aluminium is the only one which has been applied in practice. It is necessary to keep the temperature of the air or water in contact with pure aluminium below about 100° C. in order that corrosion of the aluminium itself should not occur. Hence, at the present time, energy can be extracted with water only at temperatures of about 100° C., which is much too low for the operation of an efficient heat engine. However, by extracting the heat with an inert gas instead of with water, it is probable that efficient power plants will be produced in the future. The coating on the rods serves also to keep the products of fission from escaping into the cooling air or water. The fission products, which are highly radioactive, must be kept out of the machinery, pumps, etc., which have to be serviced, and must not be allowed to pollute the air or streams of water. The amount of heat which may be extracted from uranium rods or slugs is limited also by the low heat conductivity of the metal.

The size of the pile required to obtain a reacting system is obviously very large—how large can be judged from the fact that the first such system was built up on a squash court. The pile itself must be surrounded by coatings of graphite alone, to reflect back neutrons, and the whole enclosed in absorbing walls of concrete to prevent the escape of harmful radiations. Elaborate precautions are necessary to prevent accident. Materials inside the pile become so strongly radioactive that methods of handling them from a distance become essential, and all chemical operations on the uranium removed from the system have to be carried out in such a way as to prevent injury to the operatives by radiations from the accumulated fission products. Notwithstanding all these difficulties piles have been operated at power levels of hundreds of thousands of kilowatts for several years.

The size of a reacting system can be reduced greatly by using uranium in which the concentration of the ^{235}U has been increased by partial separation of the isotopes or by adding another fissile element, e.g. plutonium, to the metal.

Not all the neutrons in the pile escape capture by ^{238}U. There is a continuous production of plutonium, the concentration of which grows until it is destroyed as fast as it is formed. This plutonium, being chemically different from the uranium, can be separated from it by chemical methods. By suitable choice of the lattice the production of plutonium can be given an optimum value. This is the method used for producing plutonium in quantity. The rate of production of the element turns out to be about 2 lbs. per day for each million kilowatts of heat energy released. All this energy is dissipated at present to heat the Colombia River!

We have indicated that a slow-neutron uranium reactor uses up the ^{235}U in the uranium rods, which accumulate fission products and a certain amount of plutonium. The fission products are a nuisance for they capture neutrons and in the end would prevent the pile from operating. They must be removed at intervals by chemical methods, and the plant for this purpose is complex and costly. After a time the concentration of ^{235}U would fall so low that the reactor would cease to operate. However, it now seems that it may be possible to replace this ^{235}U with some of the plutonium produced in the nuclear reaction from the ^{238}U.

If the number of neutrons released in the fission process is greater than 2—say 3—we might have the following balance sheet:

To maintain the chain process one neutron from each fission must be absorbed by a uranium or plutonium nucleus to produce another fission   ...   . 1 neutron.

To replace the fissionable nucleus "burnt" in the reaction a neutron must be absorbed by a ^{238}U nucleus to produce plutonium   ...   . 1 neutron.

By proper design of the reactor to reduce loss of neutrons, either from the surface or by absorption in impurities or fission products, it is possible to arrange that any excess neutrons are absorbed in further ^{238}U nuclei to produce more plutonium ...   . 1 neutron.

Thus, under these circumstances, it may be possible to produce more fresh nuclear fuel (plutonium) than is used up in the reaction. In other words a reactor may "breed" fresh reactors. Thorium undergoes a reaction similar to ^{238}U, producing a fissionable isotope of uranium (^{233}U), so that by introducing thorium into a uranium reactor thorium may be utilized in the future for atomic energy production.

The possibility of using nuclear energy for industrial purposes clearly depends upon the solution of engineering and metallurgical problems of extraction of the heat at a temperature high enough for the efficient operation of heat engines. There remains the question of the economics of the process as compared with the burning of coal or oil, and the ultimate answer to this can be obtained only by experience.

We have seen that because ^{235}U, ^{233}U, or plutonium undergo fission for neutrons of any energy, a mass of such material which is large enough will develop an explosive chain reaction through the direct multiplication of the fast fission neutrons. Plutonium or ^{233}U for the purpose can be produced in large "piles," or ^{235}U may be separated from natural uranium by one of the processes, such as diffusion of a gaseous compound of uranium through a membrane, or by means of large mass spectrographs, which have proved successful in the laboratory. Whether we require plutonium ^{233}U or ^{235}U the plant is extremely large, complex and costly.

The critical size of a fast-neutron reacting system is far smaller than that of a slow neutron system with ordinary uranium metal. The critical radius for a sphere of the material will clearly be of the order of magnitude of the free path of a fission neutron for capture by a fresh fissionable nucleus, and this is of the order of 10 cms. The critical mass must then be between 10 and 200 lbs. The critical mass will depend on the shape and the nature of the surroundings. A mass of fissile material which is smaller than the critical mass for the particular shape, is perfectly stable. If two such masses are brought rapidly together the composite structure may be several times the critical mass, and if a neutron source is then activated inside the system the whole will immediately react violently. The time of passage of a fast neutron across the mass of fissionable material is about one hundred millionth of a second, so that in a microsecond or two the number of fissions will have multiplied to a stage where the temperature has risen to tens of thousands of degrees and the pressure will have reached tens of millions of pounds per square inch. The glowing mass is far brighter than the sun itself and the radiation sears and scorches everything upon which it falls. The blast created by the expansion of the heated gases gives the great destructive effect. The neutrons emitted during the reaction destroy living cells upon which they fall, and kill human beings by destruction of the bone marrow and other active centres of the body.

Potentially, other elements than uranium and thorium can produce atomic energy. In particular, the combination of hydrogen nuclei to form heavier elements, like helium or carbon, can set free very large amounts of energy. At the present time this process is confined to the sun and stars, which are atomic energy furnaces of huge size, but it is probable that in time man will discover how to bring about this process at will. He will then possess an inexhaustible supply of power and heat for his purposes, derived from the hydrogen in the sea.

An extremely important by-product of atomic energy is the production within the reactors of radioactive forms (unstable isotopes) of practically all chemical elements. Because of the great sensitivity of the methods for detecting radioactive substances and of identifying them, these materials offer great possibilities in science and in medicine. This can best be understood by an example.

Animals and men use phosphorus, derived from food, in various ways, and especially in the formation of bone, which consists largely of a compound of calcium and phosphorus. The exact mechanism of bone formation is not known. It is not possible by chemical methods to distinguish between phosphorus already in the bones and that deposited there from a particular food. However, if we replace some of the phosphorus in the food by radioactive phosphorus, which has exactly the same chemical properties, we can now trace the course of the phosphorous through the processes of digestion and deposition in the bone, by following the radioactivity. Thus it becomes possible to unravel such important factors in health and disease as the effect of diet on the teeth. Undoubtedly we can expect a great increase in knowledge through the wise use of these radioactive "tracers" or "indicators."

It is clear that man now has at his disposal new sources of industrial power and powerful agents for research in science and in medicine. No scientist would dare prophesy what these new discoveries will contribute to man's well being in the future. It is certain that they will be used in ways which we cannot imagine at present. The development of the internal combustion engine led directly to the modern aeroplane, but Otto certainly did not envisage this when he first made his engine work. Properly used, for the benefit of man, the atomic age can bring greater comforts and better living for all, while continued research into the underlying science of nuclear physics will add to the knowledge, and hence to the cultural background and mental stature, of the men of the future. However, in order to enjoy these fruits of scientific inquiry it is necessary that the raw materials of this advance—uranium and thorium and he endeavours of men of science—should not be deviated to warlike uses. Atomic weapons are now the supreme preoccupation of all countries, and with other, and perhaps even more deadly weapons of mass destruction, render wars of the future suicidal and utterly indefensible. Proposals for the effective control of atomic energy are before the United Nations Organization, and, though negotiations have broken down, it is essential that this problem be faced, not in isolation, but as part of the problem of the elimination of war. War always was a criminal pursuit of man, but war in the future is also silly. Thinking man will surely put aside this foolishness and by positive co-operation for good ensure that "the scientific achievement" of atomic energy is a decisive step towards the better life for all.

II

MILITARY CONSEQUENCES OF ATOMIC ENERGY

P. M. S. BLACKETT

HOWEVER much disagreement there may be as to the history of the first use of atomic bombs or of the subsequent efforts to set up an international system for the control of atomic energy, there can be none as to the fact that the American stockpile of bombs is now playing an important role in present-day power politics. Since the centre of the power-political struggle in the world to-day is the threat of war between East and West, it is necessary to analyse in some detail the likely military effects of atomic bombs if a third world war breaks out within a few years, with Russia and America as the major contestants. In particular we must examine the popular thesis that such a war could be quickly and cheaply won with the aid of atomic bombs.

But before we enter into what must be a somewhat technical discussion of the effect of atomic bombs on modern warfare, it may be fitting to remind ourselves that the present epoch is not by any means the first in which the belief has been widespread that the invention of a new weapon has completely changed the character of war and rendered most previous arms obsolete. History must have seen this happen a number of times. The early sixteenth century was one of these.

In 1494, Charles VIII of France crossed the Alps and rapidly destroyed, by means of artillery and Swiss infantry, the military organization of mediaeval Italy which was based on fortified castles and the valour of the armoured knight.[1] When Machiavelli wrote his famous treatise *The Art of War*, he was much concerned to estimate the effect of firearms on warfare and to study realistically how their devastating effects could be minimized. He argued forcibly the incorrectness of the view "that hereafter all wars will be made altogether with artillery." Machiavelli's contemporary, the poet Ariosto, dramatized this threat to the contemporary order in a poem in which his hero Orlando, embodiment of all the knightly virtues, meets an enemy with a firearm. When finally Orlando had triumphed over his opponent he took the offending weapon, sailed out into the ocean, and plunged it into the sea exclaiming:

> "O! curs'd device! base implement of death!
> Fram'd in the black Tartarean realms beneath!
> By Beelzebub's malicious art design'd
> To ruin all the race of human kind . . .
> That ne'er again a knight by thee may dare,
> Or dastard cowards, by thy help in war,
> With vantage base, assault a nobler foe,
> Here lie for ever in th' abyss below!"[1]

[1] This account of the early history of firearms is taken from an article by Felix Gilbert entitled "Machiavelli: The Renaissance of the Art of War," which appears in *Makers of Modern Strategy*, Princeton 1944, an invaluable collection of studies of warfare, edited by Edward Mead Earle.

It might not be inappropriate to utter again these 400-years-old words on the hoped-for future occasion when the United Nations finally decides to consign the world's store of atomic bombs to the depth of the ocean.

Let us now jump forward in history some 400 years to the invention of aircraft in the early twentieth century. Already, in 1912, not many years after the Wright brothers first flew, air experts were writing of the devastating results to be expected of air attacks on cities.

"A military expert of high repute, speaking of the havoc that a hostile air fleet might work by an attack upon the Thames valley between Hammersmith and Gravesend, has observed: 'This whole 50 miles of concentrated essence of Empire lies at the absolute mercy of an aerial machine, which could plant a dozen incendiary missiles in certain pre-selected spots.' It was only the other day that a famous constructor showed how . . . it would be possible for an enemy to drop a couple of hundred tons of explosive matter upon London . . . What such an aerial attack as this would mean has been pictured by Lord Montagu of Beaulieu. Suppose London was thus assailed from the air, at the beginning of a war, he says: 'What would the results be? Imagine the Stock Exchange, the chief banks, the great railway stations, and our means of communication destroyed.' Such a blow at the very heart of the Empire, declares Lord Montagu: 'Would be like paralyzing the nerves of a strong man with a soporific before he had to fight for his life; the muscular force would remain but the brains would be powerless to direct.' "[1]

Such anticipations were not, in fact, fulfilled in the first world war. Aircraft played a most important, but almost exclusively a tactical role. Their main use

[1] Earle, p. 487.

was in reconnaissance and spotting for artillery, together with some light tactical bombing. The intense and costly fighter battles that developed were directed to securing the air supremacy over the battle fronts without which these tactical operations could not be carried out. German airships operated very ineffectively over England in the early years of the war, and later on a few raids were made on London by German bombing aircraft. Britain planned a heavy attack on Berlin towards the end of 1918 but the German Armies were defeated in the field before it could be carried out.

Out of these plans, however, there arose in the Royal Air Force in the early post-war years the conception of the independent use of air power against the cities and communications of the enemy, unrelated to the operation of land armies. Foremost theoretical exponent of this view was the Italian General, Giulio Douhet, whose fundamental theses have been summed up thus:[1]

(1) Aircraft are instruments of offence of incomparable potentialities, against which no effective defence can be foreseen.
(2) Civilian morale will be shattered by bombardment of centres of population.
(3) The primary objectives of aerial attack should not be the military installations, but industries and centres of population remote from the contact of the surface armies.
(4) The role of surface forces should be a defensive one, designed to hold a front and to prevent an enemy advance along the surface and in particular an enemy seizure by surface action of one's own communications, industries, and air force

[1] Earle, p. 489.

establishments, while the development of one's own aerial offensive is proceeding with its paralysis of the enemy's capacity to maintain an army and the enemy people's will to endure.

Referring to such attacks, Douhet writes:[1]

And if on the second day another ten, twenty, or fifty cities were bombed, who could keep all those lost, panic-stricken people from fleeing to the open countryside to escape this terror from the air?

A complete breakdown of the social structure cannot but take place in a country subjected to this kind of merciless pounding from the air. The time would soon come when, to put an end to horror and suffering, the people themselves, driven by the instinct of self-preservation, would rise up and demand an end to the war—this before their army and navy had time to mobilize at all!

Such an effect was to be achieved in a few days by a force of 1,500 bombers, of which only 100 were to be heavy bombers of the type used in the second world war.

At least as influential was the American General, William Mitchell, who shared with Douhet the belief that civilian morale would break quickly under air attack. "It is unnecessary that these cities be destroyed, in the sense that every house be levelled to the ground. It will be sufficient to have the civilian population driven out so that they cannot carry on their usual vocation. A few gas bombs will do that."

In future the mere threat of bombing a town by an air force will cause it to be evacuated, and all work in factories to be stopped. To gain a lasting victory in war, the hostile nation's power to make war must be destroyed,—this means the factories, the means of

[1] Earle, p. 491.

communication, the food producers, even the farms, the fuel and oil supplies, and the places where people live and carry on their daily lives. Aircraft operating in the heart of an enemy's country will accomplish this object in an incredibly short space of time.[1]

One of the chief British supporters of such a strategy was General Groves. His views have been summed up as follows:[2]

Enemy air forces would, in the future, make naval and military movements practically impossible.

Our towns would be quickly destroyed from the air and there would be no defence against that form of attack. All we could do would be in our turn to try and destroy the enemy's towns and people.

So long as our Navy and Army exist, they must be considered as being secondary to the Royal Air Force and be reduced as and when necessary to meet the requirements of the latter.

The story of the attempt of the British, German and American Air Forces to put these theories to the test in the second world war has been often told—in particular by the writer in a recent book. It will suffice here to remark that the inhabitants of London learnt to carry on the business of a great city, from which a world war was being directed and supported, under a weight of bombardment vastly greater than the followers of Douhet, Mitchell and Groves had thought would bring immediate collapse. In four years 60,000 tons of bombs and rocket weapons fell on England; 40,000 people were killed, but neither production nor civilian morale collapsed.

When the Anglo-American bombing offensive

---

[1] Earle, p. 498.
[2] Dickens. *Bombing and Strategy*. London 1946.

got into its stride, that is from 1943 to 1945, Germany took a still higher punishment from the air. In these two and a half years sixty German cities received 600,000 tons of bombs, but German civilian morale never broke, and war production rose steadily till August 1944, by which time the German Armies had been decisively defeated on two vast land fronts.

The Anglo-American bombing offensive was neither decisive nor cheap. The number of air personnel lost was 160,000—some of the best of the youth of the two countries; the loss in planes was 20,000 bombers and 18,000 fighters.

Those who remembered the senseless slaughter in the mud of Passchendaele in the first world war vowed that never would this country tolerate a repetition. In an endeavour to avoid one, we came near to staging an aerial Passchendaele in the night skies of Germany, and bolstered up our morale by a new set of self-deceptions. Where General Haig ordered all able-bodied prisoners to be removed from the cages so as to impress the visiting politicians with the desperate straits to which he believed the Allied offensive had reduced the German Army,[1] so did the British High Command delude itself and the public by bad intelligence and misleading propaganda into believing that the bombing offensive had reduced German morale and civilian economy to desperation.

Heavy aerial bombing of cities was also carried out

[1] Liddell Hart. *Why Don't We Learn from History.* 1944, p. 14.

in the war against Japan, but only in the last five months of a struggle that had already lasted forty months. In these first forty months Japan had first captured and then lost an empire—both by combined air-sea-land war not involving the attack on the civilian populations of cities. When the devastating air raids on Japan started in March 1945, they fell on a nation already essentially defeated by conventional methods of warfare. The two atomic bombs used in early August provided a way out for the ruling clique which had long known that defeat was inevitable.

A detailed study of the immediate world Press reactions to the dropping of the atomic bombs would be of great historical interest, but does not appear to have yet been made. However, the main lines of the "atomic age" which were ushered in by screaming headlines, stand vividly in one's memory. All other weapons can be relegated to the scrap heap; a small nation with atomic bombs can defeat an unsuspecting great nation in a few days; Russia has been reduced to a second-class power overnight; such were the widespread beliefs of those scared August days. Though time has brought signs of returning sanity, these themes still persist and have slipped from the newspaper headlines into State documents. America, hitherto inviolable between its oceans, might now be destroyed in a few days by atomic bomb attacks; conversely, Russia, hitherto undefeatable by the vastness of its territory, could be defeated in a few weeks. "It is we who hold the overwhelming trump cards. It is our side, not Russia, which holds atomic and post-atomic weapons and could if sufficiently provoked, literally wipe Russia's power and threat to the world's peace from the face of the earth."[1] To those who remember the prophecies of the Douhets of the early 1930's, these prophecies of the neo-Douhets of the late 1940's have a familiar ring.

Leaving aside such extreme estimates of the efficacy of atomic bombs in major wars as unrealistic, the problem remains as to how to estimate as reliably as possible the likely effect of the use of atomic bombs in a third world war between America and Russia. The only reliable method available to us at present is to base our predictions on the actual experiences of the bombing offensives of the second world war, taking into account the greatly increased destructive power of atomic bombs and making every possible allowance for the various other ways in which a third world war is likely to differ from the second.

Official American figures show that the early types of atomic bombs produced about the same destruction as some 2,000 tons of ordinary bombs evenly spread over the same area. Now some 1,200,000 tons of ordinary bombs were dropped by the Anglo-American Air Forces on Germany in the thirty months from January 1943 to the end of the war. The number of atomic bombs required to do the same damage to buildings would thus be about 600.

[1] *Observer*, June 27, 1948.

From this we can deduce at once that many hundreds of atomic bombs would have to be dropped on Russia in order to have the slightest chance of forcing a decision by air attacks alone.

If one compares such a hypothetical future atomic bomb offensive against Russia with the actual normal bombing offensive against Germany, one finds a number of different conditions which must be taken into account.

The first relates to the duration of an attack and is favourable to the atomic bomb. An atomic bomb attack could be delivered in a shorter time than it would take to drop the equivalent weight of ordinary bombs. Consequently it is often held that the total effect on morale and on production might be much greater. This is possibly so if large armies were previously poised to follow up the atomic bomb attack by immediate invasion by land. In this case a high concentration of atomic bombing in time—assuming this to be technically practicable—might be the best method to adopt. If, however, land armies were not immediately available for invasion, then clearly it would be most unwise to use the bombs at once. It would be preferable militarily to plan for a preliminary period of low intensity atomic bombing, designed to disorganize production as much as possible, lasting till the time when land armies were ready to invade, and then only greatly to increase the intensity. It is seen, therefore, that the markedly increased *intensity* of attack possible with atomic bombs is likely only to be of decisive significance in a third world war as a concomitant of invasion of Russia by land forces. If, however, the atomic bomb attack was not offensive in character, that is, if it had not the objective of forcing the defeat of Russia, but was essentially defensive in character, perhaps to attempt to stop an expansive move by Russia, then the time factor would not have such a great significance. For under these circumstances the tempo of the war would be in Russian initiative and so the advantage to the Western Powers of staging an attack, which was highly concentrated in time, would probably be small.

Another factor favourable to atomic bombing compared with the equivalent weight of ordinary bombs is the fewer sorties required and so probably the higher degree of training that can be expected of the operational crews.

The other main differences between our hypo-thetical third world war and the real second one are on the whole adverse to the atomic bomb. Some of these factors are as follows. Russia is much larger than Germany; European Russia alone being over eight times larger and the flying distance to most of the important targets is much greater. The popula-tion of Russia is over three times as large as that of Germany. The German High Command was com-pelled to improvise air defence measures, both active and passive, in the midst of a major land war, while now Russia has already had over three years in which to prepare measures against atomic bombing and, unless the Western Powers force the issue, may have many more. The heavy air attacks on Germany did not take place till she was engaged in a desperate land battle on the Eastern front in which she had already lost some 3,000,000 killed, wounded and missing.

The most effective parts of the Anglo-American bombing offensive were only made possible by almost complete command of the air over Germany. It is unlikely that this could be achieved over Russia.

Taking these arguments into account it is clear that a few hundred atomic bombs could not possibly bring quick victory in a hypothetical third world war against Russia. These arguments cannot, of course, prove that many thousands of atomic bombs might not be decisive, for there is no experience available to gauge the reactions of a nation to such a vastly destructive attack.

It is, of course, only to be expected that the American Chiefs of Staff should have prepared in some detail plans for the waging of an atomic bomb war against Russia. It is, however, somewhat surprising that General George C. Kenney, Commander of the American Strategic Air Force, should have described such plans publicly. This appears, however, to have been the case, according to a report in the American periodical *Newsweek* of May 17, 1948, from which the following extracts are taken.

General Kenney assumes that Russia will attack America as soon as she thinks she can win, and that the United States will reply to such an attack primarily by an atomic bomb attack. What would be likely then to happen is described as follows:

Although only the most extreme air-power enthusiasts still argued that planes alone could bring victory, even the Army and Navy long ago agreed that, if the Russians suddenly went berserk and swept into Western Europe, the Air Force would have to bear the brunt of the war for the first months at least.

In those initial months, the United States would have little to fight back with except the Air Force. Against the 208 divisions in the Red Army itself and the 75 additional divisions in Russia's satellite armies, the American, British, and French troops now in Europe could do little more than offer token resistance and run. Slow and ponderous as the Red Army might be, the most optimistic estimate was that it would reach the Channel Ports within two or three months. Theoretically, the Western Powers might be able to stop the Reds at the Pyrenees in Southern France or Northern Spain, and in Turkey if all the breaks went their way. The probability, however, was that within six months at the most the Hammer and Sickle would be flying over Gibraltar and on the shores of the Persian Gulf.

In the Far East the story would be the same. A few days would find all Korea in Russian hands. In three months the Red Army would be standing at the Yellow River.

What the Russians would do then, only the Russians themselves could know. They might decide to by-pass Japan and grab the Aleutians if only for the nuisance value; by landing 5,000 troops on the chain in 1942, Japan managed to keep 120,000 Americans occupied in that part of the world for months. They might decide to invade Alaska, and from it bomb the Pacific Coast. They might decide to invade Greenland to strike at the east Coast.

In any event American strategy called for securing bases around the perimeter of Russia and then striking back from the air.

The Joint Chiefs of Staff had already decided what these bases would be and, while their decision was necessarily top secret, it could only be assumed that North Africa, Japan, England and Iceland were high on their list.

Once in possession of the Channel ports the Russians would, of course, attempt to knock out England with the German V-2's which they are known to have, and with the improved rockets they are believed to have. In all probability, they would eventually succeed in making England untenable for Air Force operations. Meanwhile the Air Force would be making life extremely unpleasant for them.

This statement is of exceptional interest. Europeans will note that West Europe is treated as undefendable, or as it is often expressed as "expendable." England is expected to become eventually "untenable for Air Force operations," and so presumably also for Englishmen to live in. But before this happens it will be a useful base.

The planes would go out from England in very small groups— perhaps in twos and threes. Flying at more than 35,000 feet, they would seek to slip into Russia unnoticed. Their targets: first Moscow—Moscow above all. Then the other large cities of European Russia—Kiev, Leningrad, Kharkov, Odessa.

General Kenney states that the American heavy bomber group are still equipped with B-29 aircraft, but that the first operational squadrons of the improved types B-36s and B-50s, will be ready towards the end of 1948 or the beginning of 1949. No mention is even made of when jet bombers will come into operation, so presumably this is far in the future.

On the other hand much emphasis is put on the large number of jet fighters in use both by America and Russia. Russian jet fighters are stated to be the equal of any in the world; the Russian Air Force is said to have 14,000 operational planes, with the emphasis on fighters.

Russian radar is extremely bad, and the country's radar defences are spotty. It would be relatively easy for American planes to get across the border undetected. But in view of the excellence of the Russian fighters and fighter pilots they would face hot and heavy going once they were detected.

The likely nature of the development of such a war—after Europe had been expended—is described thus:

The United States has no intention of landing mass armies in Europe and slugging it out with the Red Army—manpower against manpower. Napoleon and Hitler both made that mistake; and Russia, with its huge population to draw on, swallowed them up. American strategists are thinking, rather, in terms of closing the circle of air bases around Russia, making it smaller and smaller, tighter and tighter, until the Russians are throttled. This means getting bases through combined air, sea and ground operations ever closer to Russia's heartland, then using the bases for sustained bombing and guided-missile attacks. The closer the bases are, the more sustained the attacks can be. Meanwhile, the Air Force will also be dropping weapons to occupied peoples behind the Red Army lines and paratroopers to help them attack the Russians from the rear.

It would be technical superiority in the air against Russian superiority in manpower. How long it would take for air-technical superiority to win is anybody's guess.

What is particularly striking about this statement is the emphasis that, even in the period before Russia acquires any atomic bombs, there is no possibility of a cheap and quick victory over Russia. This represents a distinct change from the wild hopes of the atomic-Douhets of the last three years. If General Kenney has been correctly reported and if what he is reported to have said does represent roughly the pattern of contemporary American military thinking, we may conclude that there is very little likelihood of the Western Powers deliberately forcing the present clash between East and West to the point of war.

Some further light on American strategic thinking is provided by two articles in *Life* by General Spaatz, Commander during the war of the United States Strategic Air Force in Europe and in the Pacific. In the last post he commanded the air forces which dropped the atomic bombs. In main outlines these articles resemble that of Kenney but still more emphasis is placed on the necessity of acquiring suitable advanced bases.

The first question is: is it possible to reach the vulnerable industrial system of Russia? The controlling factor now is the radius of the B-29, which with postwar improvements is more than 2,000 miles. Russia's industrial system has four centers of gravity: Moscow (chiefly light industry), the Urals and the Ukraine-Volga (predominantly heavy) and the Caucasus (oil and metal).

Take a globe and a string scaled to 2,000 miles, pin one end down at Moscow and swing the free end westward. It will take in the British Isles and part of Iceland. Swing it south and it will take in part of North Africa. Now do the same thing from the Urals, fixing one end of the string on Magnitogorsk and swinging the other south. The free end in its sweep will take in Iraq, Iran and Pakistan as far south as Karachi. From the Ukraine-Volga center the string will pass through Britain, France and North Africa. From Baku in the Caucasus the sweep will encompass part of India, Saudi Arabia and part of Europe. There is additionally in Siberia a fast-growing center of industry, not to mention the double-track Trans-Siberian railroad. This region could be reached by B-29 from China and Japan.

General Spaatz evidently reckons the effectiveness of atomic attacks on Russia higher than General Kenney, for he is reported to have written: " . . the attackers do not have to plod laboriously and bloodily along the Minsk-Smolensk-Moscow road in order to strike at Russia's vitals. Hence the war may be concluded within weeks and perhaps days."

Discounting these slight tendencies to revert to atomic Douhetism, the two Generals effectively agree that while atomic bombs do not now make a quick preventative war against Russia possible, they do constitute a deterrent against Russian expansion. If this conclusion is accepted, many extremely important conclusions follow.

If the American stockpiles of atomic bombs are looked on as the main deterrent to Russian expansion, rather than as a means of forcing her to contract her sphere of influence, then the diplomatic and strategic initiative is in an important sense handed over to Russia. For suppose that no Russian aggression, say by expansion over the Yalta line, does take place in the next few years, and suppose further that this lack of aggression is widely held in the West as due to the threat of atomic bombing, then the West will in its own view, have saved the world from a third world war at any rate for some years.

The dilemma comes later. For this policy inevitably implies leaving Russia time to make at least some atomic bombs, and when this has happened there are only three possibilities open to the West; to wage preventative war before Russia has acquired a large number of bombs, that is under less favourable military conditions than at present; to initiate a new approach to control of atomic energy on terms much more favourable to Russia; or finally to continue the atomic arms race, with a devastating atomic war with bombs available to both sides as a possible final outcome.

It is this real dilemma that exercises such a hold over many logically minded people as to lead them to become open advocates of preventative atomic war. The logic is sound, given the premise that a clash between East and West is inevitable, or that the Soviet system and Capitalism cannot exist side by side for a long time. The only escape from this dilemma is to base policy on the opposite premise, that is that a clash between East and West is not inevitable. On this view, the building up of defensive armaments by the West remains a reasonable objective, whereas the attempt to build up an offensive armament for preventative war is highly unreasonable, and is as likely as not to lead eventually to the destruction of much that is characteristic of the Western world without achieving its advertised end.

A strictly defensive policy in the West for the immediate future, to be followed as soon as possible by an attempt to negotiate an agreement with Russia while the West still holds a relatively strong bargaining position, would seem the policy most likely to achieve the objective of stopping the advance of Communism. This is not, however, the policy of Mr. Churchill who recently said:[1] "We ought to bring matters to a head and make a final settlement." "The Western nations will be far more likely to reach a lasting settlement without bloodshed, if they formulate their just demands while they have the atomic bomb and before the Russians have it too." The leading article in the London *Observer* has several times advocated a similar view. Having laid down the conditions of peace with Russia, which, following Churchill, include withdrawal to her own borders, abandonment of political subversion and economic sabotage, and acceptance of the full Atomic Energy Commission plan for the control of atomic energy, the *Observer* discusses how this is to be achieved.[2] "The only chance is to build up overwhelming strength to back our just and moderate terms of peace. Faced with overwhelming, instantly available strength, Russia might without going to war, resign herself to the position which to-day among all the nations of the world, she alone refuses —as a chess player resigns when it is clear that any exchange of pieces would lose him the game." The only possible interpretation of such statements as these is that the authors either have not read, or do not agree with the views of General Kenney, Commander of the United States Strategic Air Force

[1] October 9, 1948.   [2] November 21, 1948.

that atomic bombs do not now at any rate provide the quick and decisive weapon by which such a policy could be successfully achieved. It appears that atomic-Douhetism, already waning in influence in some realistic military circles in Washington, still survives in some political circles in London. Military realism is usually a desirable objective for any nation and at any time; it is a condition of survival for the countries of Western Europe which have already twice this century been the battlefield of the world wars and are now threatened with playing the role again in a still more devastating third one.

III

THE ECONOMIC CONSEQUENCES OF ATOMIC ENERGY

R. F. HARROD

I HAVE consented to address you on "The Economic Consequences of Atomic Energy," a subject on which I am totally ignorant. In exculpation of this seemingly conscienceless act I can plead that the difference between nescience and the knowledge possessed by the highest experts is not very great. In a subject so gravely beset with uncertainty there may be some advantages in the reflections of one who looks at the matter in an entirely detached way, free from preconceptions of all kinds.

The title naturally directs one's thoughts to the possible effects of nuclear inventions upon our standard of well-being, and to this I must address myself in due course. But I should like to begin by dwelling on certain other aspects, which also engage public attention. It is part of an economist's professional duty to interest himself in the theory of population, of upward or downward trends, not excluding the trend to zero. These trends affect, among other things, the present actuarial value of capital installations with a long prospective life. I have often heard it said that man has now at length devised a weapon whereby he may well extinguish the species. I do

not think so. I do not even think that the atomic
bomb has the highest lethal potentialities among
modern developments.

To judge this matter aright, the science which will
help us is not physics, but biology. The danger of
extinction to which I refer is that supposed to arise
from all-out atomic warfare, not from some laboratory accident. It is to biology that we should look if
we seek to learn about warfare. I understand that
internecine war is not a common phenomenon
among animals. But among humans it is of the
greatest antiquity. When the human species established itself, it was equipped with a margin of reproductive capacity sufficient to offset losses due to
internecine warfare. It is not a characteristic of this
institution that it extinguishes the species, but only
that it reduces its numbers temporarily. In war
there are victors and vanquished. The victors survive; and even the vanquished are not usually
completely extirpated. For before the point of complete elimination, the vanquished give up the battle.
This is not an accident, but of the essence of this
particular phenomenon. The vanquished lose heart
or means to carry on. Thus both sides survive. It is
reasonable to suppose that there is a causal connection
between the human surplus of reproductive poten-
tiality and the amount of loss which the vanquished
is psychologically able to endure before surrender.

I submit that this basic principle is not much
affected by whether the weapons of war are slings,
spears, high explosives or atomic bombs. It may, of

course, occur to some that as the release of nuclear energy is a revolution of unprecedented magnitude in mechanics, so it would alter the very nature of war. I see no ground for thinking that. It is possible to imagine a savage tribe of exceptionally martial ardour fighting the enemy till the last man perished. Such a state of affairs has long been impossible in modern warfare, owing to the enormously complex organization that has to be sustained behind the front line. Science has its compensations! If it has provided us with more deadly weapons, it has also ensured that it is physically impossible to fight to the last man. After a certain thinning out, that vastly complex organization on which the front line rests begins to break down. Twice we have seen the Germans, not lacking in martial qualities and fighting for what seemed to be their very existence, compelled to give way because the structure behind the lines was becoming too much deranged. Would it not be so with atomic bombs also? When the weaker side had taken a certain amount of punishment, it would be unable to sustain the organization required behind those who had to discharge atomic weapons.

I think it is important that this point should be stressed. No doubt atomic warfare would have unprecedented horrors. Yet we must not be too much alarmed. That does not serve the cause of peace. During the twenty years following 1919, we had a tremendous barrage of propaganda coming from such organizations as the League of Nations Union and from the mouths of many distinguished independent persons, depicting the horrors which another war would bring if it occurred. Yet all this propaganda seems to have been without its desired effect. The war came none the less. Indeed the propaganda may have had a deleterious effect, by inclining humane persons, their minds filled with these horrors, towards a policy of appeasement, a policy which made another war more, not less, likely. If a reasonable man thought that an atomic war, with both sides atomically armed, would extinguish the human race, then he might argue that it would be worth submitting to slavery in order to avoid war. Actually things would not so work out. In the last resort both the Americans and the British would fight *against* atomic weapons, rather than submit to slavery. The misguided notion that atomic warfare would lead to extinction might thus lead to a prolonged policy of dangerous appeasement without in the end preventing the war.

I do not wish to be taken to mean that one can use the biological argument to show that man will never exterminate himself. My argument is confined to the proposition that he will not exterminate himself by using more deadly weapons in his warfare. I fear that one has to think that it will be the greatest good luck if he does not exterminate himself sooner or later. The idea of his continuing to live for many millions of years on this planet progressing in his knowledge and power over nature, increasing his capacity and opportunity for happiness, seems too good to be true. How much more likely that his pioneering

intellect will lead him to some wayward action, bring-
ing dangers not catered for in the early days of
adaptation to environment when his species was
establishing itself. How much more likely that man
will have his day, and then give place to rats, or whatever his successors may be, to build up, through a
series of advantageous mutations, a new form of
civilized existence. I believe that we have had in our
time an invention far more deadly in its potentialities
than the atomic bomb. I refer to the contraceptive.
One can surely see at a glance what a wide difference
there is between this and the warlike weapon. New
weapons merely introduce detailed changes in the
character of an institution, which existed from the
beginning and to which we have always been
adapted. The contraceptive was not present in
aboriginal days. It is, so to speak, a new kind of
institution. It seems to me that we lack grounds for
a presumption that reproductive instincts have a
sufficient margin to offset its consequences. You
may think that I ought not to attribute the modern
low birth rate to the contraceptive alone, to the
neglect of various social and economic factors. I
believe the actual contraceptive, as produced in convenient form, to be the major cause, very largely
because it gives leaders of fashion—and I believe it
to be a small dominant minority which determines
the actions of the majority in such matters—an alibi
against the suspicion of sterility. If I am wrong, my
argument will be equally well served if for "invention of the contraceptive" we substitute "the sum of

influences which in modern communities cause the birth rate to be so low." I would like to give you figures illustrating the lethal character of the low birth rate. I quote from an earlier writing. In the first world war, which was much heavier in British casualties than the second, the United Kingdom lost in battle about three-quarters of a million men. If, during the seventeen years from 1921 to 1937 our birth rate had been at the level usual before 1870, about fifteen million more children would have been born in England and Wales alone than were born there during those years. "Thus in the smaller area we lost, through the lower birth rate, twenty times as many lives in seventeen years as we lost in World War I—more in each year than in the whole war (although perhaps war losses should be doubled to allow for the fact that women were sterilized through the loss of men)."

We may put the matter in another way. I do not believe that we could continue fighting until one-quarter of our population (about twelve and a half million persons) had been killed by atomic bombs. Yet even if this happened, we could, by having a birth rate at the level usual before 1870 and modern methods of infant care, make good the population in thirty years.

I do not want to minimize the havoc wrought by war. There is no doubt that the elimination of war would be far the greatest possible contribution to human progress. How much higher our standard of living would be now, had we been spared two world wars! It may be noticed in passing, however, that the loss of wealth due to unemployment in America and elsewhere after 1929 was probably considerably greater than that due to the first world war. Nor do I want to minimize the vast increase of havoc that would be entailed by an atomic war. I merely wish to guard against misconceptions embodied in such phrases as "the end of the human race," or "the end of civilization."

To avoid misunderstanding I must add that while I do not believe that atomic bombs will lead to the extinction of the human race, Professor Blackett in his recent book on the *Military and Political Consequences of Atomic Energy* appears to have erred on the other side. I cannot reconcile his calculations with the fact that one single bomb dropped on Hiroshima killed considerably more persons than the whole of the German attack by bombs and flying bombs upon Britain. No doubt we must introduce some factor to allow for the peculiarly vulnerable condition of the population of Hiroshima, but whatever we allow, this fact seems entirely inconsistent with the view that it would take four hundred atomic bombs—and there may be more powerful ones—to produce as great an effect on the enemy as the Allied bombing attack inflicted on Germany. This must surely greatly overestimate the effect of our air attack on Germany, which, however, Professor Blackett regards as "a costly failure."

And since I have mentioned this book, which deals with matters affecting our vital interests so deeply, I must be allowed a further comment. Professor Blackett suggests that a policy of armed neutrality might be advantageous to Britain. It is important that the widest possible protest should be made against such a suggestion. The arguments do not depend on Professor Blackett's elaborate conjectures regarding the course of a future war but relate to the situation here and now. The interest of the United States in the defence of Western Europe depends entirely on her being able to count on unequivocal and solid support from Britain.[1] If there were any serious doubts about Britain's attitude, the United States would have to alter her whole strategy in the direction of abandoning interest in Europe and relying upon the Atlantic ditch. It is not a question of paper agreements or commitments; it is a question of confidence; the United States, if she is to base plans for the defence of her own people on an advanced base in Europe, must feel that Britain can be relied on implicitly to behave honourably and with vigour in this matter. If she could not do this and had to abandon the idea of such a strategy, on the following day Russia would begin by an inexorable process to seep forward and acquire control up to the Atlantic coast. There is no need to impute a base motive. From the point of view of ordinary self-interest, especially after her experience in 1941, she seeks the best possible means of defence, and from a more

[1] The fact that such a commentator as Mr. Lipmann is capable of taking a low view of British solidarity in the good cause shows our danger clearly—see passage cited by Mr. Blackett, p. 185.

altruistic point of view, she may deem that her system of government, which she compares with Tsarism, would be a benefit to the peoples of Europe. She cannot understand, nor could she necessarily be expected to take the matter into her reckoning if she did understand, that the establishment of a Russian-dominated communism would involve the extinction of all that is most precious in Western European civilization.

And where would Britain be then? We may imagine Russia in due course, as Mr. Blackett suggests, making a collection of atomic bombs. She would have the resources of Europe and half Asia at her disposal. Britain by her policy of neutrality would have rendered herself unable to rely on outside support. Against such overwhelming odds, a fight for liberty would seem hopeless. Professor Blackett gives grounds for thinking that there may not be a war between the U.S.A. and the U.S.S.R. in the near future. But this consideration is irrelevant. Britain would go under without any such war. So long as the United States is interested in Western Europe, Britain will only come into great troubles if there is a war between these two Powers; but on Professor Blackett's plan, she would be doomed in any event.

Nor, even at the price of slavery, would she escape the horrors of atomic war. For, as a matter of fact, however desperate the position, however forlorn the hope, she would fight for her liberty. The atomic bombs would rain down. The United States might even then, despite Britain's base policy of neutrality, seek to come to her aid; but in the circumstances envisaged, with no joint preparations made, it would probably be too late. Thus Professor Blackett's plan would prepare for Britain an inevitable death by violence. He repeats the mistakes that were made in the period before Munich, with consequences infinitely more disastrous.

If we are thinking of the end of civilization, I am inclined to regard the cost of preparation for atomic war as a greater danger. I am not thinking of the manufacture of bombs, rockets, etc., but of defence. There is said to be no defence against atomic bombs, but does not this only mean that the defence would be very costly? If we were really, facing an atomic attack, thought to be probable, we should not be content to be devoid of defence. The first thing that comes to mind is dispersion. This is terribly costly. The trifling amount of dispersion we had in World War II added substantially to our burdens. Radical dispersion would greatly lower our productive capacity. Modern industrial organization requires concentration. Incidentally, we should probably lose the greater part of our countryside.

And would people be content with dispersion? Even Professor Blackett's neutrality is to be an "armed" one, and he speaks of the benefit of shelters. Might it not be deemed necessary to go underground, especially for vital services, such as the manufacture of atomic weapons themselves, of aeroplanes, etc.? The trouble is that in modern warfare, the greater part of industry is indispensable. Far-reaching schemes for going underground would be intolerably costly. In addition to the excavation, there would be the immensely elaborate gear needed to decontaminate the atmosphere before it came into the air conditioning system. I imagine that if such tasks were undertaken, we should have to undergo austerity of living quite unprecedented. Civilization would indeed be at an end. This is a serious debit consequent upon the possibility of atomic warfare, probably more destructive than the horrors of the war itself.

I now come to the credit side. Owing to my ignorance, which I do not attempt to conceal, it may be expedient to take refuge in a logical classification. I classify the possible benefits under five heads. The first four relate to the provision of goods and services that we think we need and have hitherto enjoyed, albeit in insufficient quantity. Sub-dividing again, the first two suppose a substitution of atomic power for other forms of power, the old methods of production being otherwise broadly unchanged. The other two are concerned with radical changes in methods of production. I am concerned in this list only with the use of power and heat. Other uses of radio-active substances, e.g. for medical purposes, may be separately considered. I come to my list:

(1) There are the economies which might arise by the substitution of cheaper atomic power for other forms of mechanical power, coal, oil, etc., now in use.

(2) There are the economies due to the possible

substitution of atomic power where human or animal power is now used.

(3) There are the economies in methods of production which might be facilitated by the more convenient form in which the new power was presented for use.

(4) There are the economies which might arise from the use of massive cheap power to facilitate radical changes in methods of production.

(5) There is the possibility of the provision of new goods and services hitherto not enjoyed by man.

I believe that in considering these possibilities we should have in mind that industrial progress has not consisted mainly in the cheapening of power for productive purposes. There have, of course, been very essential milestones in our advance which were connected with power. The substitution of mechanical power from coal for human and animal power was of course fundamental. The convenience which is provided by the portability of oil was an important step. But after the introduction of steam power, our main lines of progress have been in engineering, whereby we achieve ever greater dexterity and economy in changing the shapes of materials, and in chemistry, whereby our knowledge of the properties of matter is increased, so that a whole series of new substances can be produced.

Under the first head I will first make the extreme hypothesis that atomic power and heat could be rendered wherever required more or less free of cost. This is not likely to be realized! It would then be possible to substitute this power for other forms of mechanical power now in use. What would be the gain to our standard of living? I suggest that for a country like Britain (or the United States) the gain would be trivial. In order to provide a broad quantitive estimate, it is not necessary to go into meticulous detail. I suggest that in Britain the maximum increase in our national income, on this extremely favourable hypothesis, would be under 6 per cent. I arrive at this figure as follows:

At mid 1948, 674,000 men were engaged in getting coal; add 337,000 (50 per cent of former) for producing all the gear required in coal mining; add 100,000 for those transporting coal by rail. We have a total of 1,111,000 engaged in supplying mechanical power. This is 5·83 per cent of the total in civil employment. I may have omitted certain small items of labour; I have omitted the cost of oil, which is comparatively small, on the ground that cars are not likely to be driven by nuclear energy; there is the industrial use of oil, but against this it is certain that some coal will be needed, e.g. for metallurgy; on the other hand, the fraction of our national income due to the group which I have counted is probably smaller than the fraction of all employed constituted by it. When we take into account the fact that I am assuming that the provision of atomic power would cost nothing, it cannot be argued that I am minimizing the saving in cost. In a more elaborate and realistic calculation for the United States, Dr. Marschak reaches the conclusion that the saving would only be from 1 to 2 per cent of national income. What we have experienced in many decades suggests that we may expect the national income to rise by at least $1\frac{1}{4}$ per cent per annum. Thus, under this head, the provision of atomic power gratis would merely enable us to jump forward in our normal industrial progress by some $4\frac{1}{2}$ years. This is clearly trivial. Who could possibly suppose that this modest benefit was worth having at the price of all the political complications which the equipment of atomic power plants would entail in international relations? There may, of course, be places such as the Sahara desert where other forms of power are remote and the saving in transport would be greater. I pass to the second head.

Would very cheap power justify its substitution in many processes which are now performed by human muscle? This does not seem a very promising line. The obstacle to substituting a mechanical process for a hand process is not usually the cost of the power, but the cost of the mechanism required. It is often said that Britain is woefully backward in the installation of mechanical handling gear at many points in the industrial system. This is by comparison with the United States. It is not clear why the United States is so far in advance of Britain; some hold that it has been lack of initiative on the British side. But the United States has made the advances it has, despite mechanical power costing what it now costs. The question is, would the United States introduce large additional substitutions of mechanical

E

for human power if the cost of the former were greatly reduced? I do not know the answer to this question, but I cannot believe that the economies under this head would be nearly as large as under the first head. If that was true, they would be trivial indeed.

The third heading is much more difficult, and it is one on which we await information. I have already pointed out that it is under this head that the great advantage of the development of the internal combustion engine has lain. On the whole it does not seem likely that atomic power would come to us in a highly convenient form. The favourite example of the experts, when questioned, is the use of atomic power for the propulsion of ocean-going vessels. I do not know if it is claimed that the construction of "atomic vessels" would be much cheaper than that of those propelled by oil. Re-fuelling would be less frequent and the turn-round of vessels expedited. They might go more quickly. That would be an advantage, although we must not exaggerate it. On critical occasions such as a war in which we have to make a sudden great adjustment in our shipping arrangements, the cutting down of the time of a round trip might be an immense boon. That is because we suddenly have to impose large new tasks on an existing fleet. But when, as normally, the size of the mercantile fleet is adjusted to requirements, the benefit is much smaller; it is, to be precise, the interest on the value of the ship's cargo during the time saved. Interest rates in these days are running fairly low. Nor would there be any special advantage in another war, because the total size of the mercantile fleet would meanwhile have been adjusted downwards in relation to peace-time needs to offset the quicker turn-round.

It is difficult to believe that, generally, the atomic energy will be delivered in a form that greatly simplifies productive processes. There will be the appalling problems of safeguarding personnel and disposing of waste products safely. All this is not very "convenient".

Possible savings under the fourth heading are the most speculative of all. It is here that we particularly need expert guidance. If, but only if, atomic power were very cheap, it might be used massively and thereby revolutionize productive processes. Under this head it is not a question of doing by atomic power what was formerly done by other forms of mechanical power or human power, but applying much more power to primitive substances and thereby lessening or simplifying the processes by which these substances are converted into consumable commodities. For instance, if power were very cheap, our land might be heated up and made to yield more abundant crops. This is not as hopeful as it seems. It is a fallacy to suppose that it is intrinsically advantageous to increase the yield of a given piece of land. If the crops grown have subsequently to be put through the same processes as before, the only saving (apart from some modest labour-saving in the work of harrowing, etc.) is in the amount of acreage required. This might be deemed very advantageous for Britain by those who fear she will prove unable to buy cheap food from abroad, as formerly. From the point of view of the world as a whole it is not very advantageous, unless one postulates that it is desirable that the world should sustain a vastly greater population than there now is. I have already expressed myself on the evil consequences likely to flow from very low birth rates. It does not follow that we need be in favour of an immense multiplication of the human species. This is clearly a deep philosophical question. There is at least no hurry to reach a definite conclusion, or postulate that it is a good thing to go ahead with a vast increase. Failing that, the intensification of production from certain lands would enable us to dispense with "marginal lands" on which costs were higher. The savings would not be of an order of magnitude which could be deemed to constitute a revolution in human well-being. Furthermore, I understand that it is not clear that available quantities of uranium—even if we throw in thorium—are sufficient to enable us to sustain the application of massive quantities of heat all the world over. We have, at our disposal, a most excellent power plant for nuclear energy stationed in the sun, at a safe distance so far as lethal by-products are concerned. May it not be rather foolish to endeavour to undercut it at competitive prices?

There may, however, be various ways in which massive power could be applied to initiate wholly new methods of production. That is where we seek guidance.

Finally, there is the fifth heading. Under this we may let our imaginations run riot. The quantity of conceivable new services may be without limit. But if one is concerned to assess solid benefits that may be set against the undoubted disadvantages of the development of nuclear power, one should look extremely critically at this item. It might be very amusing to have various new forms of activity, but one must remember that they would be rival to existing forms and that the net advantage may be doubtful. The advantage of "stimulating new needs" has long been a matter of controversy. I am not myself the enemy of that modest expenditure on advertisements that we have, which has been widely condemned, because, by stimulating new needs and offering to satisfy them, it merely wastes resources. There is something to be said for "new needs." But one should be chary if they involve grave countervailing detriment. Man is not really short of needs! He already has a multitude of ways by which intellectual and bodily cravings may be satisfied, if only he had time and leisure for them. New ways are not so much required as the opportunity for exploiting existing ways. For those capable of higher intellectual and aesthetic appreciation there are the vast worlds of philosophy and science, of literature and music. How many there are who would gladly devote more of their lives to these pursuits, if only they had sufficient leisure. It may be argued that there is only a proportion of humanity to which these delights appeal; this is a doubtful point. But even if it can be argued that there is a large proportion who can only fulfil their higher natures by the more homely forms of self-expression in love and personal relations and that this more "lowbrow" section needs new forms of diversion in leisure, I would urge that in games of all sorts there are boundless possibilities, if only they could be exploited. I reject the view that in the foreseeable future man will have no satisfying way of filling his leisure hours and needs such new forms of diversion as might be provided by the development of massive power. I hold that the fifth heading may be left completely out of our reckoning.

I come next to a totally different kind of argument in favour of nuclear development. It is said that it would be "good for trade." Under the five headings already considered, we have been concerned with possible improvements in the standard of living. This is the fundamental aspect of the problem. The attribute of being "good for trade" is secondary and relates to existing economic arrangements, which can always be altered. I shall show that precisely to the extent that this secondary advantage can be claimed, if it can, it negatives the primary advantage.

The argument rests on the supposition, with which I agree, that in the developed countries, particularly the United States, we may reach, after post-war adjustments have been fully carried out and supposing that a new armaments race does not gather excessive momentum, a phase of "stagnation."

An essential freedom is the right of the individual to save part of his income against future contingencies. In countries where average incomes are high, savings are likely to be great. Hitherto, at least before 1914, it was easy and profitable to devise various forms of productive equipment in which these savings could be embodied. The savings of each man, viz. the excess of the value of his production over what he chose to consume were aggregated and made available for increasing the nation's stock of productive appliances. The savers became, in fact, the owners of these appliances; thus the titles to wealth were embodied in physical form and carried forward in the direct or indirect ownership of the savers, always capable of being disposed of when these wished to release and enjoy the fruits of their past excess of production over consumption. Recently it has begun to appear probable that a surfeit of appliances was occurring and that there would not each year be a sufficient number of new appliances to mop up the savings. The main reason for this has been the slowing down in the increase in population tending towards a stationary condition; for it is the increment of population which constitutes the main demand for additional appliances. When savings are not mopped up, industrial depression and unemployment occur. The consequent loss in a country such as the United States was comparable to that due to a major war.

The argument is, therefore, that the appliances required for nuclear development would be a happy windfall, since they would provide a use for savings and thus keep the economy stimulated to the full employment level. It may be noted in passing that this argument, while applicable to the United States and perhaps to the United Kingdom, by no means applies to the more backward areas where there is plenty of development on more old-fashioned lines still due, and where the trouble is deficiency rather than excess of savings. It has been pointed out that the excess savings of the maturer communities might be used to help the backward ones; and within limits, that will no doubt be done, although there are political difficulties, on grounds both of security and of the unwillingness of backward nations to be entirely bought up by the richer ones, and the development of backward countries is limited by the quality of the personnel available in them.

There is no doubt that the nuclear development would be a stimulus to trade of the kind suggested. What should concern us is how important it would be in quantity. If the stimulus were a relatively small one, it would not absolve such a country as the United States from taking other measures to solve the "stagnation" problem. If the stimulus were a large one, on the other hand, it might solve it for a generation, and this, of course, would be an advantage. The cost of the two bombs that were discharged together with all the preceding development has been stated to have been $2 billion. This must be compared with the national income of the United States, which has been running at about $200 billion. Owing to violent fluctuations both since and before

1939 it is difficult to gauge what fraction of this $ 200 billion, the citizens of the United States will normally be prepared to save. Pre-war figures are no guide because the national income was severely depressed and saving was small. Indeed it was thus depressed precisely because there was not vent for a larger quantity of saving and the economic system kept the national income down to a level at which people would not save more than was required. During the war, savings were naturally very high. Recently private savings have been running in the neighbour-hood of $10 billion. One should perhaps add some $5 billion for corporate saving. It may be that this sum understates probable future saving since people in the United States, as here, have been making good arrears of consumer goods. Thus we have to compare the $2 billion which the bomb cost with an annual flow of funds of some $15 billion, perhaps, seeking investment. What would be the cost of full-scale atomic development? If it was of the order of a hundred times the initial cost, viz. $200 billion, spread out over some thirty years, then that would certainly be a substantial contribution towards the disposal of surplus savings. On the other hand, if the plants were indeed so costly, that would be incon-sistent with the idea of cheap power. Taking 5 per cent on $200 billion for interest and amortization, we should have a charge of $10 billion a year, and that would not mean cheap power for the United States. Thus, if the nuclear development is to have good marks for being a substantial contribution to the state of trade in the United States, it cannot be deemed to be likely to make much contribution to the standard of living. The more it is praised on the secondary count, the more it loses on the primary and more fundamental count.

I confess that the rudimentary analysis which I have given leaves me somewhat sceptical. A true appraisal of the cost of nuclear energy would greatly reduce the benefit of less than 6 per cent as computed under the first head; we cannot yet be sure that it would not reduce it to zero. Benefits under the second head are likely to be trivial and benefits under the fifth head I rule out entirely. There remain the third and fourth heads. Such pointers as we have had do not suggest great benefits under the third head and the main open question is under the fourth head.

Now if some decision has to be made in the years immediately ahead, it appears to me that it would be wise to discount possible benefits under the fourth head until we know more. Decisions made now could be reversed later when research had yielded better information. I confess that I am inclined to be sceptical about the alleged economic benefits to humanity, anyhow in this generation. I have the idea that certain encouraging and hopeful statements that emanated from the world of scientists in the early days after Hiroshima may have been due to the promptings of a guilty conscience.[1] The eyes of the

[1] Among those within my cognisance I must make an exception in favour of Lord Cherwell, who stated the opposite view in the House of Lords as early as October 16th, 1945.

world were directed upon scientists with looks of reproach. What was this new ghastly scourge which they had inflicted upon humanity? It was natural that scientists should be anxious to make the best of the other side, both from the point of view of their own self-esteem and, more important, in the interests of science itself. It is desirable that the average unscientific man should not look with disfavour upon scientific progress. Science needs money and goodwill. If one result of scientific research appears baneful, there is some tendency for the whole of science to fall into disrepute. Vast though the benefits which it has conferred upon mankind have been, the ordinary man is apt to take them for granted and forget their provenance. Ardent trade unionists, for instance, attribute the immense improvements in the standard of living of their members to their successes in collective bargaining! Once the fruits of deep research have become a matter of daily routine, they are taken for granted, as though vouchsafed, like the sunshine, in the ordinary course of nature.

If the economic value of the development of nuclear energy is still in doubt, we ought surely, in the present state of the world, to be willing to call a standstill, if that would have manifest benefits. At least the position should be examined from this point of view.

You will excuse me if I venture in my concluding section somewhat outside the terms of my title. Indeed, I think it would be wrong to withhold from the forum of discussion certain ideas I have reached on this momentous topic.

We are all aware of the present deadlock. I have suggested that if sufficient goodwill is lacking among the nations to remove the possibility of atomic war, we may well be led into defensive preparations of most destructive costliness. In them almost more than in such a war itself, I see a menace to the continuance of civilized life.

At present our attention and our irritation are focussed upon Russia. In this phase the suspicion entertained by that nation seems the greatest obstacle to progress. I have no doubt that there are certain nations which would not in any event use atomic weapons for aggressive purposes in any foreseeable future, but there are also other nations. As the decades and generations go by, we do not know what tyrannies may arise. Where there is political instability, the goodwill of the main mass of people is no guarantee of a permanent peaceable disposition on the part of their government. What new tyrannies may not in due course arise among the 2,000 million people on this globe!

The main obstacle to a satisfactory settlement in the mind of a nation which has suspicion of its neighbours is the dislike of excessive interference by an international body in its internal affairs. There is also the fear of revealing an imperfectly filled cupboard! The suspicious nation has an unconquerable aversion to having an international cadre, a body of malign aliens as it seems to it, penetrating deeply into its society. Such penetration is inevitable if there is to be a thorough-going control over mining and over the various power plants that may be set up. Detailed processes throughout the plants must be under minute inspection and control, if diversion to improper use is to be made impossible.

The aversion of the suspicious nation cannot be regarded as a foible which can be removed by some friendly conversation. I conceive it possible that those formidable persons who control the fate of Russia may have repeatedly asked themselves in all earnestness and sincerity, whether it would not really be in their interest to subscribe to the kinds of schemes that have been put forward. And I conceive such promptings towards international co-operation being overcome by an unconquerable and irresistible inhibition against allowing foreigners to penetrate deeply into the secrets of the economic life of their country.

But suppose it were now decided to suspend completely all development of the use of nuclear energy for industrial as well as for warlike purposes. Suppose that it were decided that in no country were there to be any power plants at all. In order to enforce such an international agreement, if it could be obtained, rigorous inspection would still be necessary. No one would be content with a paper agreement without the guarantee provided by mutual inspection. But surely the inspection then required would be of an altogether different and far milder character. It would only be necessary to make sure that these gigantic plants were not being erected. A minute territorial inspection would indeed be needed as a security against subterranean works. But I conceive that such an inspection of the superficial area of a country would be far less vexatious to the suspicious Power than the installation of an international cadre inside the works themselves. The more the use of nuclear energy became an integral part of the industrial structure of the country, the more knowledge and thereby the more control the international cadre would have to have in relation to the whole productive system of the country. On the other plan its knowledge would be mainly negative; it would have to assure itself of the absence of mammoth installations of a certain type. No doubt it would be very vexatious to have foreigners walking about one's country at all. But surely this would be much less vexatious than their having the right to control certain establishments and to understand the quantity and character and purpose of the forms of power required to be produced by them. They would have to keep track of everything that went in and out of the gates. Would it not be worth while at least to experiment with this alternative idea? It might well be that the Russian reaction would be quite different. While I have held the views here set out for a considerable time now, I have pleasure in drawing your attention to their similarity to those of a much more competent authority, namely, the Working Committee of the Association of Scientists for Atomic Education, Atlantic Region. These were embodied in a proposal addressed to the Atomic Energy Commission on April 2nd last.

It is not possible to legislate now for the whole future of the human race. If we had a standstill agreement for twenty or thirty years, the matter could be reviewed in the light of international relations as they then were. With time, an easement may come. On the other hand, with the present pressure to adopt an unwelcome expedient, exacerbation is increasing. Would it not be well to require the International Energy Commission to work out in detail precisely what forms of inspection would be required on the assumption that the use of nuclear energy for industrial purposes would be forsworn by all.

I conceive that such a standstill agreement would not be inconsistent with the retention of piles of moderate size for the provision of materials for research and for hospital work.

Furthermore, if it was thought desirable to have some fancy scheme, falling under my fifth heading, such as a journey to the moon, that could be segregated in an island and supervised by an international authority. On such an island it might also be possible to make various experiments in the development of power, whereby one might get a close assessment of what the economic benefits of the use of this power would be.

Indeed practical experiments in the use of power for industrial purposes on such an island might be a feature of my programme of general prohibition. The International Authority would not use the island as an arsenal of bombs, as envisaged in early thinking about this matter. Each nation would have to be able to assure itself that, in the event of a *coup de main* by some power in seizing the island for the abuse of its resources, it had severally and independently of international agreement, a means of totally destroying the installations at a minute's notice.

May I summarize my conclusions? While no doubt humanity would gain some advantage in the diversion of nuclear energy into power for economic purposes, it is not at present *a priori* probable that the advantage would be great. If one allows the creation of power for economic purposes in the various countries, its creation for warlike purposes can only be prevented by a very thorough-going and oppressive system of international control. Unhappily international relations are now such as to make it unlikely that nations will consent to this. I suggest that the proposal should be put forward that all nations should agree to forgo the use of nuclear energy for the generation of industrial power for a term of years. I suggest that the Atomic Energy Commission should be asked to formulate precisely the nature of the inspection that would be needed to secure the enforcement of this agreement. It might well prove to be the case that this far milder form of inspection would be acceptable to all the nations.

IV

VALUES IN THE ATOMIC AGE

BERTRAND RUSSELL

THE invention of atomic bombs has been a cause of very considerable moral perplexity, and of a new realization of the dangers of international anarchy.

I do not myself feel that there is, in principle, any *new* ground for moral perplexity. War has always been horrible, and it is no new thing for its worst sufferings to fall on the heads of innocent non-combatants. A hundred years ago the bombing of cities with ordinary bombs, which is now taken as a matter of course, would have been regarded, if someone had prophesied it, as a fantastic horror which its victims would never endure, and which could never be inflicted except by fiends wholly lost to all feelings of humanity. But we get used to things which, at first, are rightly viewed as abominations. It has turned out that every nation at war is willing to bomb enemy civilians, and that civilians everywhere can endure bombing without loss of morale. Shall we in time get used to atom bombs as an ordinary incident of warfare? I hope not, but my hope is not a very confident one.

Among those to whom moral issues are important there has been much debate as to whether the use of atom bombs in war is ethically justifiable. I think

F

myself that this is not the right way to put the question. If war occurs, both sides are sure to do all they can to achieve victory. If they do not think victory of sufficient importance to justify their doing so, they ought not to go to war. The question should not be: "Is it justifiable to use atomic bombs when there is war?" But: "Is it justifiable to make war when atomic bombs are sure to be involved?" I do not think this question can be answered in the abstract. Given a very important issue and a rather small number of bombs, I think that even atomic warfare may be justified. But it seems extremely probable that, if great wars continue till the end of the present century, the number and destructiveness of atom bombs will increase to a point at which the evils of war will be of quite a new order. It is this consideration that makes it imperative to seek a new political system that will make great wars very unlikely to occur.

In its abstract form, the problem we have to consider is this: Can we preserve what we think of value in our civilization while creating the kind of organization that is necessary if wars are to be prevented? Or, if we cannot preserve everything that we think of value, what must we do in order to preserve as much as possible? And taking the more hopeful side of our problem: if a system which will prevent war can be created, what new goods, now unattainable, will it make possible?

I will state in advance the conclusion to which I have been led in considering this problem. I think that, if our scientific civilization is to survive, it will be necessary to submit, at any rate for a century or two, to a very considerable loss of liberty, especially national liberty. I think that this will have various depressing effects which I regard as profoundly regrettable. Throughout history the great ages in the lives of nations have been those in which they were adventurous: Aeschylus is an outcome of Salamis, and Shakespeare of the defeat of the Armada. But in the new world in which we must henceforth live or perish, the price of adventurousness is too high, and a more humdrum type of virtue is, for the present, an indispensable condition of survival.

There is, however, another side of the picture, which is far more cheerful. At present, all except the most thoughtless live under the shadow of FEAR. The future is so uncertain that it seems futile to provide for it. The young have so much doubt as to their own survival that many of them feel it useless to live seriously, while others are driven to an evasion of painful realities by various kinds of pleasant phantasy that unfit them for coping with the problems of the actual situation. If this shadow of fear can be dissipated, there will be a revival of hopefulness and vigour and power to enjoy life without dangerous illusions. All this is possible, though not, I fear, in the *immediate* future. I do not see how the immediate future can be other than painful, but I shall try to persuade you that there are wholly rational hopes which, if we keep them alive in our thoughts, will make the pain less unendurable.

After these introductory remarks, I come now to the detailed consideration of our problem.

Political circumstances, however grave they may be, can make no difference as regards fundamental values, but only as to what it is possible to achieve. If you hold, for example, that happiness is to be valued and that pain is an evil, your opinion, if it is true at all, is true always. There may be times when happiness is very difficult to achieve, and when the main endeavour of the social reformer must be confined to diminishing unhappiness. But this is a judgment as to what can be done, not as to what would be good if it could be done. What changes according to circumstances is the possibility of securing this or that good thing, or diminishing the amount of this or that bad thing. It would be a waste of time and effort to pursue wholly impracticable aims however desirable they might be. If you hold, for example, that death is an evil, you might be led to further medical research with a view to increasing longevity, but you would realize that death cannot be abolished, and that therefore, even if it be an evil, it must be endured. So, in the situation in which the world is at present, it is useless—at any rate so far as the near future is concerned—to aim at certain good things which not so long ago seemed possible of attainment. My aim in this lecture, accordingly, will be to inquire what evils the atomic age has, for the present, made inevitable, and what new goods, if any, it has made possible.

I think the changes brought by the discovery of

ways of utilizing atomic energy are in line with a
transformation which has been going on ever since
the industrial revolution. Scientific technique has inevitably increased the amount of organization in the
world, and the interdependence of different groups
upon each other. It has followed from this that indi-
viduals or groups are more capable of doing harm to
others than they were at an earlier age, unless their
anarchic or destructive impulses can be restrained
by law. War is perhaps the most notable example of
this, but by no means the only one. Strikes and lock-
outs and refusals to supply essential raw materials
can, in our time, cause dislocations which would have
been impossible in the eighteenth century. And apart
from any criminal or malevolent impulses, the mere
increase in the density of population necessarily
diminishes the degree of unregulated liberty that is
compatible with an ordered social life.

In the early nineteenth century the principal aim
of reformers was liberty—liberty of the individual
from governmental tyranny, and liberty of nations
from alien domination.

Individual liberty had first been successfully established in the religious sphere, though only after 130
years of fruitless religious wars. Religious toleration
only became possible when war-weariness had so
abated the vehemence of both sides that governments
no longer had to fear plots and assassinations on the
part of fanatics. Until that stage was reached, it was
natural that more stress should be laid on security
than on liberty. Now that the atmosphere has again

grown like that of the sixteenth century, the doctrine of ideological toleration, which to our grandfathers seemed absolute, is explicitly repudiated by communists, and subjected to various limitations by their opponents.

When the battle for religious liberty had been won, Liberalism embarked upon a campaign for personal freedom in the economic sphere. The doctrine of *laisser-faire* swept away a host of mediaeval regulations and restrictions, and in England won a resounding victory over mercantilism. Like other creeds, this creed had its fanatics. These fanatics, for example, opposed the Public Health Act of 1848, on the ground, one must suppose, that the individual has an indefeasible right to create insanitary conditions which may cause his neighbour's death. Parliament, in theory, agreed with these fanatics. But there were violent epidemics in the slums of Westminster, which, in those days, and still when I was young, came close to the Houses of Parliament. When Honourable Members realized their own danger, theoretical scruples gave way, and intelligent measures for combating disease were permitted.

From the earliest Factory Acts down to the minute regulations of the present day, there has been a continually increasing renunciation of the doctrine of *laisser-faire*. It was felt to be a travesty that in the name of liberty children should be compelled to work in factories for twelve, fourteen, or sixteen hours a day, and through this small breach in the walls of dogma the invading armies of mercy and common sense gradually penetrated. What may be broadly called Socialism has consisted, in the main, of a substitution of security for liberty as the guiding principle in regard to economic activity.

The champions of *laisser-faire* were, in the main, hard-headed practical men, who imagined themselves destitute of illusions, and, like Mr. Murdstone, took as their watchword the precept: "No weakness!" It was a softer and more sentimental school of Liberals that took up the cry of *national* freedom.

The question of national freedom is more germane to our theme than the older questions of religious and economic freedom, but I have wished to recall these others because I think we can trace in all three a similar movement from unwise regulation to freedom, and thence to a new and wiser kind of regulation. And in all three cases the growth of freedom has been due to the diminution of old dangers, while its subsequent restriction has been due to the growth of new dangers. In relation to national freedom the movement towards new restrictions is still at an early stage, but it is my contention that it is as necessary as the restrictions which have had to be imposed on economic *laisser-faire*.

The doctrine of national freedom lent itself, as Adam Smith did not, to expression in poetry and rhetoric. It was inspired by the heroic memories of Marathon and Thermopylae, King Alfred and William Tell and Joan of Arc. As expounded, for instance, by Mazzini, it held that every man is a member of some national group, to whose members he feels a mystical affinity which enables him to co-operate with them more completely than with those who belong to some different national group. The Rights of Man become, in this sphere, the Rights of Nations: a government should be co-extensive with a nation, and every nation should be "free." If several nations co-operate voluntarily, well and good, but no nation must be *compelled* to co-operate with another, still less to obey another.

It is obvious that there was a very considerable measure of truth in this doctrine. It was absurd that Italians should be subject to the Hapsburgs, and that Germany should be divided into a multitude of petty States. It was unjust that Poland should be par-titioned, and that the Balkans should have to suffer Turkish misrule. In all these cases the creation of national States might be expected to increase the happiness of the populations concerned.

But the dogmatic adherents of the principle of nationality, like the dogmatic adherents of *laisser-faire*, closed their eyes to a number of problems. In the first place, most of them thought only of Europe. Should the Arabs be freed from subjection to the Turks? You may search the poems of Byron from end to end without finding any allusion to this ques-tion, in spite of the fact that for him the Turks are always the villains of the piece. Should India be freed from the British? Should white imperialism in Africa be condemned? Were the Zulu nation and the Basuto nation mystic entities like the German and

Italian nations? On such subjects the principle of nationality, in its early days, was silent.

In the second place, the more advanced nations had certain claims that were felt to be valid, however they might conflict with theory. Suez and Panama had an importance for the world's shipping which made it impossible to leave them to the unrestricted sovereignty of those who happened to live in the neighbourhood. Important raw materials, such as oil, could not be left unexploited because of benighted local opposition. In questions of this kind practice was inconsistent with theory, although the theory was not explicitly abandoned.

There was a third objection to the principle of nationality, which, though psychological rather than logical, turned out to be of great practical importance. Although, in theory, every nation might be held to have equal rights, it was natural to suppose that oppressed nations were morally superior to their oppressors. A nation rightly struggling to be free would have no doubt as to its own nobility. The energy, self-confidence, and self-laudation developed during the struggle inevitably turned, in the moment of success, into oppression of any minority group within the liberated nation and aggression against any foreign nation which seemed easy to defeat. "To have character and to be German," said Fichte, "undoubtedly mean the same thing." This sentiment was designed to secure self-preservation against Napoleon, but it led straight on to Bismarck, William II, and Hitler. It has been a fairly general experience that the virtue of oppressed nations ceases when they cease to be oppressed, and that most of them, given the opportunity, are eager to wreak upon others crimes exactly like those of which they were formerly the victims.

In spite of these objections, the principle of nationality became incorporated in the doctrine of liberalism, just as *laisser-faire* had been at any earlier date. The supreme moment of its practical success was at the end of the first world war, when President Wilson caused it to be applied in a manner which the second world war showed to have been somewhat reckless. In the modern world, a nation which is small cannot be self-subsistent in a military sense, and can only be self-subsistent in an economic sense at the cost of a very considerable material sacrifice. I say this is true of a nation which is "small," but which nations are "small"? This depends upon the state of military and economic technique; as both advance, larger and larger nations must count as "small." There are now only two States which are not "small," namely Russia and America. All the rest are incapable of self-preservation by their own efforts, and cannot therefore be completely independent in fact, whatever they may be in law.

Nineteenth-century reformers, for the most part, valued above all things LIBERTY, both individual and national. While fully admitting the value of liberty, we must, in the world as it now is, lay more stress on SECURITY. The trend towards security, as we have seen, is by no means new; security has been one of the chief aims of socialism as opposed to liberalism. But the security that socialism sought was economic, and the liberty that it restricted was individual, while the security that must now be sought is military, and the liberty that it must restrict is national. I shall endeavour first to prove the necessity of such restriction, and then to consider whether there are any ways of achieving what is necessary before disaster overtakes the human race.

The first thing to realize is the practical certainty of wars if nothing drastic is done to prevent them. I am not thinking specifically of a third world war in the near future: I am thinking more generally. So long as there are a plurality of sovereign States, each free to develop its own armaments, it must be regarded as in the highest degree probable that, from time to time, there will be disputes that each side will consider too important for compromise. This has always been the case throughout history, and will presumably continue to be the case until some new institution makes war on a large scale impossible. There are some who hope that wars will be brought to an end by men becoming more rational, or more virtuous; such hopes seem to me visionary, unless as a result of measures causing a long period of peace, during which mental habits might be changed. Neither reason nor virtue will prevent war, unless one or other dominates *all* the powerful governments of the world, and I do not see any ground for expecting this in the near future.

There are those who think that war may be

prevented by the realization of its horrors. Nobel
thought this would be the result of the invention of
dynamite, and many people thought, at first, that it
would be the result of the atom bomb. In fact, however, every increase in the expected horrors of war
makes war more likely, not less. War is promoted
by suspicion and fear. Suppose some well-meaning
pacifist were to suggest to Americans that they had
better conciliate Russia, because otherwise suit-
cases containing atom time-bombs may be deposited
in stations in all the principal cities of America,
and by their simultaneous explosion may destroy
America's capacity to fight before it is known that
the war has started. Would belief in this possibility really promote peace? Is it not obvious that,
on the contrary, it would immensely stimulate anti-
Russian feeling, and probably lead to a preventive
war? Powerful nations do not like to be bullied,
and are ashamed of yielding to fear. I do not
think, therefore, that the atom bomb has done anything at all to diminish the likelihood of war, so
long as the present system of international anarchy
persists.

We must, nevertheless, do our best to make a
rational forecast of the prospects for mankind if
great wars continue. This is a very conjectural
matter, and one as to which competent authorities
differ very widely. I note, however, that, on the
whole, those who know most about nuclear physics
are the most gloomy in their prophecies.

The harm that can be done by atom bombs in

moderate quantities depends upon the density of the population. England or Belgium could be quickly crippled by destruction of its cities and munition centres; so could a concentrated industrial area such as the Ruhr. Large countries with room for dispersion would be much less vulnerable. If there is a war within the next few years, it seems probable that the ultimate decision will still depend upon large bodies of infantry, though atom bombs (if only one side has them) may greatly impede the production of munitions, and may interfere with lines of communication by making crucial areas dangerously radioactive. The destructiveness of such a war would differ only in degree, not in kind, from that of the two world wars that we have already enjoyed.

The further outlook, however, is much more serious. It is to be presumed that in a fourth world war both sides would have atomic bombs in large numbers, and no doubt with much greater destructive power than those employed at Hiroshima and Nagasaki. Apart from immediate lethal effects, there would be lingering diseases and perhaps sterility. Considerable areas could be rendered for many years uninhabitable. Probably crops could be destroyed on a large scale. And we must not forget the hitherto untested possibilities of bacteriological warfare. In such a world of danger, destitution, and death, populations would develop mass-hysterias which would complete the havoc wrought by the enemy. It is not improbable that ordered government would cease, and that the war would end in a welter of marauding bands armed only with such primitive weapons as could survive the destruction of munition centres.

This picture, however, errs, if it errs at all, on the side of optimism. If it were all that we have to fear, mankind might, in a thousand years or so, restore civilization and again become capable of scientific suicide. It may be that this will be the outcome if atomic wars continue, but there is another possible outcome which is worse.

It is true, as Mr. Harrod said, that nations will not deliberately fight to the point of extermination. But atomic forces are to some degree incalculable, and may have unintended effects.

If atom bombs are used in large numbers—as is to be expected if great wars continue—it is thought by some nuclear physicists whose opinion commands respect that they are likely to generate radioactive clouds, which will drift with the wind, and destroy every form of life as they pass, leaving our planet, at the end of a few years, completely destitute of both animals and plants.

We cannot console ourselves with the thought that Uranium 235 is a very rare element, of which the supply may be exhausted before the human race has come to an end. If a way is found—as it probably will be if civilization survives for another fifty years —of synthesizing heavier elements from hydrogen, it will be possible to liberate explosive forces ten times as powerful as those now available. And for this process the raw material will be water, of which the supply is virtually inexhaustible.

It seems, accordingly, that if scientific warfare continues much longer, there is some reason to fear that Man is doomed. Since all human goods depend upon the existence of human beings, we shall be wise to accept even quite considerable evils if they are the necessary condition for the abolition of war.

There are only three ways of preventing the continuation of scientific warfare. The first is the extinction of the human race; the second is reversion to barbarism; the third is the creation of a single government with a monopoly of armed force. Perhaps an impartial outsider, if there were one, would, like M. Micromégas in Voltaire's fable, incline to the first solution, on the ground that mankind have proved themselves unworthy to exist. But we are not impartial outsiders, and I shall assume that you agree with me in not regarding this solution as wholly satisfactory. The second possibility, reversion to barbarism, is no real solution, since in time men would again become "civilized" and be able to bring about a second cataclysm. It remains to consider the possibility of the third solution, namely the creation of a single armed force sufficiently powerful to police the world and keep in subjection the anarchic impulses of *homo sapiens*.

Let us first consider the question in a purely abstract manner, without regard to the facts of the present international situation. Modern weapons are so powerful that, if one armed force had a monopoly of the most formidable among them, resistance to it would be futile, and would, if it occurred, be crushed quickly without the need of large-scale destruction. In such circumstances, the only possibility of serious war would be a clash between rival factions within the world army. This possibility must be borne in mind; it is one that can only be averted by political means calculated to prevent mutiny.

The efficacy of a world army, considered solely in relation to the prevention of war, does not depend upon the way in which it is constituted, provided its cohesion can be relied upon. It might be an army to which every nation would contribute in proportion to its population; it might represent a victorious coalition; or, finally, it might be the national army of a State which had achieved world empire. Corresponding to these possibilities, the political power to which it would owe obedience might be a voluntary Federation of the World, or an Alliance of certain States, or one supreme Power. In any of these cases, the one army would be equally effective in preventing war.

The existence of a single world army will only prevent war if the army has a reliable loyalty to some political government. If not, there may be civil wars between rival claimants to supreme command, as in the Roman Empire. Obedience of armies to civil governments is a modern achievement. It did not exist in England in the time of Cromwell or in France in 1799. In the United States in early days, and even during the Civil War, there was some fear of a military dictatorship. In modern times the politicians have had little to fear from armies. Forcible seizures of power, such as those by Lenin, Mussolini, and Hitler, have not been primarily military. The supremacy of the politicians depends upon psychological factors: it would have been impossible in 1945 for a Conservative General to lead his troops against the newly elected House of Commons, because they would have refused to follow him. Somehow, this loyalty to the civil government must survive if the single armed force is to afford security against war.

I come at last to the question: in the world as it is, what likelihood is there of the unification of armed force, and by what stages is it most likely to be achieved?

There are at the present time many advocates of world government. The great majority of them, in the West, think of it as brought about by agreement among the nations, and as in a greater or less degree democratic. I have no doubt that a world government of this sort ought to be our ultimate aim. No one is more firmly persuaded than I am that agreement is better than force and democracy is better than imperialism. But I do not see at present any prospect of world government by agreement. Time presses, and if utter disaster is to be averted the unification of the world's armed forces must be effected within fifty years at furthest. If the matter is left to the slow course of diplomatic debate and popular propaganda, it seems unlikely that it can be accomplished in the time at our disposal, for we

G

must not forget the possibility that universal death may overtake us while we are still debating.

The first step, though by no means a sufficient one, has been thought to be the internationalizing of atomic energy. For this step all nations have expressed their willingness except Russia and her satellites. But Russian opposition is apparently insuperable. Argument at the governmental level has been tried in vain, and appeal to popular opinion is impossible wherever communists are in power. Unless the Soviet Government changes its mind, which does not seem at all likely, I am afraid we must conclude that no approach to unification will be possible until after the next world war.

In saying this, however, I am making an assumption which must be examined. Someone may say: since the dangers involved in war are so great, and since unification is so essential, why not submit to communism and allow it to acquire control of the whole world? It might be a sufficient answer to say that such a suggestion is not practical politics. The Western world will not accept communist dictatorship except as the result of defeat in war. I should like, however, to add that in this I think the Western world is in the right. If—what I devoutly hope is not the case—only war can prevent the universal victory of communism, then I, for my part, would accept war in spite of all the destruction that it must involve. And in this I believe the great majority in America and Britain would now agree with me.

Let us suppose the conflict of Russia and America

resolved, either by a Russian change of policy or by
an American victory in war. There would still remain
difficulties in the way of world government by agreement, and these difficulties would be so great that I
see no reasonable hope of their being resolved within
a generation. If each State is to count equally, the
United States will have only half the nominal weight
of an alliance of Nicaragua and Guatemala. If, on the
other hand, each State is to count in proportion to
population, the United States will have only a third
of the representation falling to China. Neither plan
would be acceptable to the United States. It is clear
that the most powerful States will expect to have
their preponderance of power recognized in the
Constitution, but that States which, like China and
India, are populous but not well armed will resent
such a claim. Many of the difficulties are familiar,
since they stultified both the League of Nations and
the United Nations. But there are others which, if
any approach to democratic equality were attempted,
would become very grave. The United States, Australia, and South Africa would all resist Asiatic immigration, but pressure of population would lead Asia
to demand this as a right. I do not see how any
democratic governmental machinery can deal with
problems of this sort.

A world government, if it is to serve any useful
purpose, must be stable, and it will not be stable
if its constitution does not, in some degree, reflect
the real balance of forces in the world. If a party
which is numerically in a minority has an obvious

preponderance of military strength, it will have a constant temptation to appeal to force when it is outvoted, and if the issue is felt to be important it will succumb to this temptation.

There are moreover large regions where the population has not as yet the political education required for democracy. In such regions, the attempt to impose democracy prematurely can only lead to either confusion or dictatorship, as well as to loss by the industrially developed nations of raw materials which they will not willingly forgo.

For these among other reasons, I hold that a democratic world government, or any world government brought about by voluntary agreement, while it should be our ultimate goal, cannot be our immediate aim. Some other way of preventing war must be found if our civilization is to survive.

In view of the above difficulties, there is, so far as I can see, only one way in which mankind can avoid unparalleled disaster, and that is by the world-wide hegemony of a single Power. If one State, if possible as leader in an alliance, becomes strong enough to compel those others that might be dangerous to forgo serious armaments, the unification of armed forces which we have seen to be necessary will be brought about. Moreover, it will be brought about by processes that are in line with normal human desires and do not require either heroic self-sacrifice or a love of humanity only to be expected of saints. The paramount nation will act in accordance with nationalism, and the power motive will reinforce its necessary activities, since its own sovereignty will not at first be essentially restricted. In any *voluntary* association of nations involving a partial surrender of sovereignty there will always be a reluctance to go far enough, a desire to reserve crucial questions, and a difficult process of haggling when compromise decisions are necessary. Moreover, in the international army it is to be feared that national loyalties will persist, making civil wars not unlikely. Such dangers are avoided if the army is national, and if decisions in the international sphere do not need ratification by many different States. I should hope that, if a world war should break out and if the United States were victorious, America would, at the end, retain its monopoly of atomic bombs, and make economic assistance to possibly hostile nations dependent upon a radical reduction in their armaments.

All this, I know, is repugnant to liberal sentiments, and to the national pride of nations whose history has been long and glorious. It is only the blackness of the alternative that reconciles me to such a prospect.

The liberal dislike of imperialism, which I consider entirely just, need not be wholly inefficacious, even under such a system. In the first place the paramount Power should be only the leader in an alliance, and should exercise only such controls over other nations as are necessary for the prevention of war. In all other respects national liberties should be respected. In the second place the United States and

its allies should offer to admit to the alliance all
nations willing to agree to certain terms, and thought
likely to abide by their agreement. By this means,
in no very long time, the original imperialistic unification of the world could be transformed, step by
step, into a voluntary federation.

If once the peace of the world were secured, even
by such a method as I have suggested, so many fears
would vanish from people's lives, so many old habits
would decay, that the substitution of co-operation for
domination would become much easier than it looks
at present. But at no stage in this evolution must
liberal sentiment go so far as to relax unitary military
control. There must, throughout, be only one armed
force unquestionably loyal to a single civil authority.
That authority I conceive, at first, to be the government of the Alliance in which the United States is
paramount. When step by step it is enlarged to admit
other nations, the process must be sufficiently gradual
to make it possible for a genuine loyalty towards the
Federation to grow up. For unless there is such a
sentiment the whole system will be unstable.

I suggest that this way of unification is one which
the course of events is quite likely to bring about,
whereas all other schemes for world federation that
I know of are in some degree Utopian, and postulate
on the part of large populations actions which seem
contrary to normal political impulses. The situation
is, after all, closely analogous to what happened in
national states in the fifteenth and sixteenth cen-
turies. The anarchic barons would never have

voluntarily forgone their turbulent independence. It was the power of the King that compelled a unification which, with the lapse of time, ultimately made democratic government possible. I think the international anarchy must be dealt with in the same way, by enlisting the power impulses of the strongest nation, not by hoping for rational agreement among all the nations. If, however, that strongest nation is the United States, as there is every reason to expect, we may hope that its exercise of power will not be tyrannical beyond a point, especially as the United States will be acting in concert with important allies. Undoubtedly we shall at times sigh for the old unrestricted freedoms, but I do not think that our lot will be one hundredth part as bad as if we attempted to preserve those freedoms in a world which has grown too dangerous for them. To this extent, in my opinion, the dangers of the atomic age compel us to modify our adherence to certain of the values upheld by nineteenth-century liberalism.

And when we think of things other than freedom we find that there will be immense compensations. There could be an almost total cessation of fear in many forms in which it now oppresses mankind. There could be, within fifty years or so, an almost complete abolition of poverty throughout the world. There could be an immense increase of leisure, of education, and of opportunities for artistic creation. No longer would parents have to wonder, in watching their children, whether they were doomed to a premature death in some frantic holocaust. No longer

would all effort seem no more than a vain endeavour
to escape from inevitable disaster. No longer would
the feeling of living at the end of an epoch sap men's
creative energies and drive them into folly or irra-
tionality. If once the awful problem of war has been
dealt with, even if the method be somewhat rough,
so great a weight will be lifted from the human
spirit that we may hope for a new breath of creative
hope and a new leap forward in the whole life of the
human species.

V

THE POLITICAL REPERCUSSIONS
OF ATOMIC POWER

LIONEL CURTIS

In his essay Lord Russell propounded the thesis
that "fundamental values are unaffected by political
events." I agree so strongly that all that I have to
say to-night on the political repercussions of atomic
power will be based on Lord Russell's thesis.

Previous lectures in this course leave an impression
that the release of atomic energy is the greatest
achievement which science has yet attained.

Inventions to which such discoveries lead have
had various objects. Explosives were invented to
destroy life, but in modern times have been used for
the service of man in making tunnels, mining,
quarrying and other useful works. The steam engine
and the internal combustion engine were invented to
serve human welfare, but were quickly adapted for
the purpose of war. The atom was split by physicists
whose minds were set on the search for knowledge;
but the first invention to which their discoveries were
applied was a bomb more deadly than any weapon
before invented. From the lectures we have heard,
one sees with what consternation physicists regard
the first use to which their greatest discovery has
been put. They are now set on discovering how it can

be used to add to the happiness of men instead of destroying them. In order to do this, some way to prevent its use in war must be found. We are thus facing the political repercussion of the bombs dropped on Hiroshima and Nagasaki.

In September 1947, the report of a group on atomic energy was published by Chatham House. The introduction ends with the following words: "The matter of supreme importance is that the world at large should be brought to realize that it stands at the parting of the ways, that decision cannot be indefinitely delayed, and that, even while it is pending, the possibilities of ultimate disaster from the misuse of science are growing day by day. This report is issued in the hope that it may contribute to the awakening and the enlightenment of public opinion as to the supreme importance and the extreme urgency of this world problem" (page 13).

The United Nations Organization has lost no time in considering how to control the use and study of atomic power. The Chairman of the group which reported to Chatham House on this subject was Sir Henry Dale, President of the British Association, and from 1940 to 1945 President of the Royal Society. In his opening chapter of the report, Sir Henry Dale makes the following comment: "Much of the procedure involved in preparing to use atomic energy as a source of peaceful power is identical with and, in practice, inseparable from that which is required to obtain fissile materials for use in instruments of war. A large part of the duty of an inspectorate under any effective system of international control would, therefore, be to ensure that installations ostensibly concerned with the generation of power were not in fact covertly diverting fissile products to the preparation of atomic weapons. A plan to exempt from control and inspection any plants not admittedly concerned with atomic energy reduces an international authority to impotence" (page 26).

It was clear from the outset that no effective control is possible, unless the controlling authority, which must, of course, be international, has power to inspect any establishment in the world in which it was thought that atomic energy was being applied for the purpose of war. The controlling authority must also have power to employ force, if necessary, to prevent such use.

All such proposals were vetoed by Soviet Russia, which thus brought to a standstill any further discussion of the problem at Lake Success. The U.S.A. is, I believe, the only country which at present possesses atomic bombs and the full means of making them. How long it will be before other countries acquire the knowledge how they are made and plant for making them is a matter of conjecture. If a war breaks out in which the U.S.A. is involved, widespread destruction of human life will ensue. If war breaks out when a number of states are equipped with this weapon, it is likely to end civilization and may even imperil the existence of life on this earth.

We have thus to live in expectation of catastrophe on the same universal scale as the day of judgment, in which I was taught as a child to believe. In that awful day a just God would send the great majority of men to everlasting perdition. Only the righteous few would be saved. The followers of Calvin believed that nothing that mortal men could do would avert their predestined doom.

In this age when few of us think that a God of Love could ordain such a fate for men made in His likeness, such a day has now been prepared by man for himself, a day in which the righteous and wicked will perish together. How men of a former age would have smiled if anyone had broached an idea so fantastic! We have, however, this one consolation. There is nothing which men could do to avert the day when "the heavens would depart as a scroll that is rolled together; and every mountain and island would be removed." To prevent the destruction of life on this earth by atomic energy rests in our own hands. We can master our fate when, in mastering nature, we learn how to master ourselves. But such mastery is not achieved by incantations of pious words, but only by those means whereby physicists have released atomic energy, by giving effect to imaginative thought in practical measures.

Not seldom the good which new inventions were meant to do has been more than undone by the evil purpose to which they were turned. The internal combustion engine is a case in point. The world would, on balance, be happier than it now is if motor-cars and the aeroplane had not been invented. All the good they have done has been more than

outweighed by submarines, tanks and bombers, because our power to control physical forces has increased out of all proportion to our power to control
human forces. Our problem now is to enable society to
establish control over itself. To do this we have
first to see how far men are able to control each
other.

The world is divided into more than sixty States,
in each of which a national government maintains
varying degrees of order. To this end each government exacts the obedience of all who are in its territory and can exact it so far as a sufficient number of
its subjects are prepared to enforce its commands.
If enough of its subjects are not prepared to enforce
the commands of government, the weak then lie at
the mercy of the strong, government ceases to exist
and gives place to anarchy, a Greek word which
means there is no government. A government can
only exist where enough of its subjects are ready,
when called on to do so, to give their lives to enforce
its commands. All governments claim this unlimited
obedience from all their subjects. They claim
sovereignty. That is a fact: by ignoring that fact
philosophers have brought society to the verge of
destruction.

I am not here concerned to say what sovereignty is,
but I am concerned to say what I myself mean when
I speak of sovereignty. I mean that every government claims the right to exact obedience from all its
subjects.

In the nineteenth century the idea of sovereignty

was deeply influenced by the views of the jurist Austin. Sir Henry Maine said of those views, "They are indispensable, if for no other object, for the purpose of clearing the head." Austin said of himself that "his special vocation was that of untying intellectual knots."

In his article on Austin in the eleventh edition of the *Encyclopaedia Britannica*, printed in 1910, Sir William Markby writes: "He began lecturing in 1828, and at first not without encouragement. His class was a peculiarly brilliant one. It included a number of men who afterwards became eminent in law, politics and philosophy—Sir George Cornewall Lewis, Charles Buller, Charles Villiers, Sir Samuel Romilly and his brother Lord Romilly, Edward Strutt—afterwards Lord Belper, Sir William Erle and John Stuart Mill were all members of his class. All of these have left on record expressions of the profound admiration which the lectures excited in the minds of those who heard them."

The article ends with the following words: "It is a curious reflection that whilst the lectures in which those inquiries were begun excited the admiration of his contemporaries, hardly anyone now thinks such inquiries worth pursuing."

Now how did this happen? In Austin's view there is in each state an authority competent to over-rule every person or corporation within its jurisdiction and to enforce its rule if necessary. Such a view, stated in the absolute terms of one whose object it was to clear people's heads, was agreeable to authoritarian rulers in Europe. Dr. Otto Gierke, an Austrian who resented the claims of the Austrian Empire to sovereign authority, wrote a book on *Political Theories of the Middle Ages* in which he challenged the assumption that a government is entitled to over-rule all other authorities such as churches, corporations, trade unions and so on. The tendency of his book was to reduce the Government to a footing of equality with other corporations or groups. The question how conflicts between various groups can be settled, when agreement has failed, has always been evaded by Gierke and his followers. At Cambridge the doctrine of Gierke appealed to Figgis, an Anglo-Catholic, who questioned the right of the state to over-rule the claims of the Church. It caught the fancy of the eminent jurist Maitland who in 1900 published an English translation of *Political Theories of the Middle Ages* with an introduction abler than the book which it introduced. "The set of thoughts," he wrote, "about law and sovereignty into which Englishmen were lectured by John Austin appears to Dr. Gierke as a past stage."

That the influence of German thought on legal and educational circles in England was then at its height is recorded in a phrase common at the time that "What is not German is not germane." The word "Austinian" became in political language a term of abuse, more deadly even than the word "Hobbesian."

The translation of Gierke's book, together with Maitland's introduction, set a fashion of thought in

Universities wherever the English tongue is used. Books like *The Federalist* fell into disuse, even in the United States. *The Federalist* was the work of Alexander Hamilton, Maddison and Jay, whose thought had been the major influence in shaping the constitution of the United States in the Congress of Philadelphia. It reflected the mind of Washington, who presided over the Congress. In the Supreme Court the judges who interpret the constitution refer to it as an authority second only to the text of that constitution.

In 1938 I addressed teachers of history and politics at Canadian Universities from Vancouver to Montreal and then to a similar gathering at Harvard. I always began by saying that I did not want to waste my hearers' time by telling them about a book which they had all read. So I asked that if anyone had not read *The Federalist* he would hold up his hand. At every meeting about 90 per cent of those present held up their hands.

On returning to Oxford I addressed men and women teachers in a lunch club confined to teachers of leftish outlook, with the same result. In a gathering of nearly forty, only four had read *The Federalist*.

Some years earlier, when at Johannesburg, I was talking to an American officer of health who had been successful in protecting the labourers employed on the Panama Canal from malaria. He was then engaged by the mining industry to combat the incidence of pneumonia which was decimating the native labourers in the mines. In the course of our conversation he observed that the medical profession was always dominated by one fashion or other. Some time ago the ruling fashion had been to remove the appendix. "I now spend my time," he said, "dissuading friends not to submit to the operation for duodenal ulcer." "There is one profession more subject to fashion than yours," I said, "the profession which teaches politics, history and law." The fashion of thought set by Gierke, Maitland and Figgis explains the fact that in the audiences of teachers I addressed in 1938 only 10 per cent had read *The Federalist* which is, I should say, one of the two or three most important books on politics ever written.

How far this fashion has gone was brought home to me during the war by a letter I received from a leading teacher of politics who had read a pamphlet I had just published. In this letter he said, "I should like to see you fined £5 every time you mention the word 'sovereignty'." When I showed the letter to another such friend who happened to be present when I opened it, he said, "The only point on which I differ from that letter is that I should make the fine £10." I told the story to an experienced government official who remarked, "If only these good people could spend a day in a government office, they would find that everything it does rests on the assumption that behind the office is an authority which claims the right to over-rule every other authority in its jurisdiction."

In those words he enabled me to say exactly what

H

I mean when I use the word "sovereignty." I do not presume to say what sovereignty is, but only what I myself mean when I use the word. Nor do I presume to discuss the question raised by George Fox, Tolstoy or Gandhi, whether such a claim is morally justified. I confine myself to the fact that the claim *is* made by every authority which deserves to be called a government in the fullest sense of the word. To treat that fact as a figment and to deny it is to ignore the most vital of all political facts. And that is what the latter-day followers of the fashion set by Gierke, Maitland and Figgis are now doing.

If we are to deal with the problem set by the release of atomic energy, we must first look at the facts, and then at opinions with regard to them which experienced scientists and public men have given us.

The outstanding fact is that, under the charter, the Council of U.N.O. can do nothing important unless the U.S.A., Britain, France, China and Soviet Russia are agreed.

In his opening chapter of the report on Atomic Energy issued by Chatham House, the Chairman of the group, Sir Henry Dale, referred to the offer made by the U.S.A. as follows: "The spontaneous offer made by the Fèderal Government of the United States to transfer to an international authority the whole of that nation's property, at present unique, in the plant, material and knowledge required for the production of atomic energy, must be recognized as an act of enlightened generosity without parallel in the whole history of international dealings" (page 24).

The spokesman of the Soviet Union refused to commit his government to any measure of international control until the U.S.A. had first surrendered the dominant position she now holds by reason of the fact that her experts alone know how to produce the bomb, and surrendered the plant to produce them, upon which she has spent billions of dollars.

It is useless to hope that Russia will ever agree to any effective plan for controlling the study of atomic energy. We need not break our hearts over this if we agree with Lord Hankey that any plan for control which depends on the continuous agreement of the Powers is more likely to lead to war than if things are left as they now are. I must, therefore, give in his own words what Lord Hankey said on this subject in the House of Lords on February 18, 1948:

"The big question is whether effective control is feasible. That problem still remains, and I should like to examine it a little. Effective it must be, for nations will not give up research and production of atomic bombs, and other war uses of atomic energy, unless they are satisfied that an absolutely reliable scheme of control is available. An unreliable scheme is worse than no scheme, because it gives all the advantages to the aggressor.

"I am afraid that the schemes upon which the Atomic Energy Commission have worked do not inspire much confidence in that respect. It is easy to draw up a paper scheme on the assumption that all the nations will sign and ratify the Treaty; that all will play the game; that there will be no running out when they have got the 'know-how'; and that the whole of their territories will be thrown open. At present a great many territories, including the whole of Russia, are not thrown open. Nations must be willing to throw open the Government offices where there are documents, plans and suspected agreements with other countries, or their own plans for making the bombs secretly. They have to throw open the arsenals, magazines, dockyards and anywhere where they could hide either the raw material or atomic energy in any form. It is also easy to draw up schemes on the assumption that there will be no espionage, no bribery, no corruption, no attempt to conceal or mislead; that none of the hundreds (perhaps thousands) of persons engaged in the inspection and control will put the interests of his own country before those of the United Nations; and that none will be open to those tendentious influences which we saw in the case of the Canadian Royal Commission, influences through which men and women of apparently high standing, selected for responsible positions and entrusted with national secrets, were gradually 'drawn into the net'—the phrase which is constantly used. If we make all those assumptions, we may assume that war itself can be abolished; and *I am not at all sure that it is not easier—or at least any more difficult—to abolish war than it is to find a really reliable control which the nations can trust.*

"Let us pause for a moment to consider the

personnel who will be employed and the conditions in which they will carry out their work. They will come from many countries—a fact which always weakens loyalty and team work—for every nation will want to have a finger in the pie. They will also want to get the 'know-how' of atomic energy, especially in the early days when the scheme is still on probation and the secret not yet divulged. Is it not certain that some countries will plant the organization with agents, whose business it will be to discover all the secrets in order to forward the interests of their own countries rather than those of the United Nations? Then let us consider the inspectors of this varied personnel, planted out all over the world in different countries for years at a time, in dull places, with the hateful task of ferreting out the evasion of the rules, whether it be in mine, laboratory or factory, or on the communications between the two. Will they really be able to carry out their task? Will they be allowed to see more than their hosts want them to see? Some nations are past masters in gulling people. I suggest that the inspectors will often be gulled or lulled into inactivity and into keeping their eyes shut.

"In the vast spaces of America, Asia or Africa—to look very far ahead—how are these inspectors to discover what is going on? Will these territories be open to them? Why, nobody is even allowed to fly over some of them! What chance or hope is there of agreement until we get over that kind of difficulty?

"However ingenious a scheme is, if a nation wants

to break it I am afraid they would be able to do so. There will be no means of enforcing control upon a strong recalcitrant nation, or group of nations, except by a world war, and it would be very difficult to get anyone to face that. I think we knew that the Germans were breaking the Naval Treaty but there was not much we could do about it. If a major war breaks out, and the whole matter of agreements is washed out, then within a year or two, I am afraid, all the nations will have the bomb. It seems to me that any nation would be mad to entrust its security to any scheme which has been produced up to the present time."

I find the opinion of Captain Cyril Falls, Professor of Military History at Oxford, that if war breaks out the atom bomb will be used, not less convincing. We have before us the opinion of great physicists, including experts who produced the bombs dropped on Japan, that the use of these bombs will destroy civiization and may even end by destroying all human life on the earth.

According to Sir Henry Dale, "Other atomic weapons, of destructive power vastly greater than these, may certainly be expected if the situation continues without remedy; nor is it by any means certain that atomic energy will ultimately provide the nations with the most effective means of destroying one another, if the discoveries of science in all directions continue to be at call for such perversion.

"There is no likelihood that any useful measures of defence will be found against atomic bombs, or against more effective weapons of mass destruction which other applications of science may yet provide; the only 'defence' would apparently be in priority of annihilating attack" (page 27).

I think that Professor Blackett has made an unanswerable point when he argues that, even if the United Nations Organization could control the release of atomic energy, it would still be impossible to control the bacteriological destruction of whole nations. In his book (page 174) he quotes Lord Cherwell as saying "Germ warfare has the unpleasant characteristic that it spreads catalytically; a few germs in favourable circumstances may go on generating more and more. Modern poisons are excessively potent; one pound of them properly distributed would be enough to poison the whole of the inhabitants of the globe."

When scientific experts like Sir Henry Dale and Lord Cherwell warn us that the nations who live in mutual fear will presently have the power as well as a motive to poison each other wholesale if war recurs, is it not time to face the truth that in order to save civilization and perhaps our very existence we must see to it that war never happens again? When Lord Hankey questions whether it is possible to control the use of atomic power for mass destruction he adds "I am not at all sure that it is not easier to abolish war." These words from one who has played a major part in preparing to fight and in fighting the two greatest wars in history are significant of the change of outlook that the threat of atomic and bacteriological warfare is forcing on politicians as well as on soldiers.

Having won two wars, we now live in hourly fear of a third. In order to win the peace we had best consider how we won the last of those wars. In this second war, as in the first, the American people hoped to keep out of it, but when their fleet in Pearl Harbour was sunk by Japan without warning, it was realized that no democracy can now keep out of a war which has once started between major powers, by virtue of its own strength, however great. The United Nations, when joined by the U.S.A., pooled their forces under one command, and in three years won the war at incredible cost, by reducing the great cities of Europe to ruins. Had they pooled their forces ten years before, the general staff was then strong enough to have stopped Hitler from going to war, the Nazi regime would have fallen and the crisis would have passed. There would have been no second war in 1939.

It is equally clear that if the democracies pool their forces in peace as they pooled them in war, there will be no third war. I am glad to find that Lord Russell and I agree on this point, that war can be prevented so long as states based on freedom, keep themselves too strong for any aggressor to attack. This was the truth spoken by Mr. Dewey in his memorable speech at Salt Lake City.

The solution is as simple as that, but I do not mean that it is easy because it is simple. When bombs were dropping on land, ships were torpedoed at sea, and utter destruction was staring democracies in the face, they were ready to follow the leaders who saw that the only way to avoid defeat was by pooling their forces. But in war every government knew that when the victory was gained, they would then recover control of their national forces. Their national sovereignty was only suspended till war had been won. They would then regain it.

In order to pool their forces in peace under one government, the democracies must first create a government to organize and control those forces for the common defence. To create such a government they would have first to obtain the assent of electorates but this they could not do either at a general election or by a referendum, until they had agreed on a constitution. In submitting this constitution to the voters they would have to tell them that, by accepting the constitution, they would merge their national sovereignty in an international union, and that such a decision would then be irrevocable. Their national sovereignty could never be regained except by a civil war, that is to say, by defeating the very object for which the union had been made. We have thus to recognize that the whole problem rests on the question of sovereignty, which, as I have said before, is the vital fact of the situation. If we are to deal with the repercussions of atomic power, we must begin by merging national sovereignties in an international sovereignty. Here again I am glad to find that Lord Russell and I agree.

Sir Henry Dale closes his first chapter with the following words: "No such possibilities could come

into view, however, without agreement on the
requisite surrender of national sovereignty; and this,
if once conceded, might provide a first step towards a
world government of international relations under
the United Nations, with abandonment of all military
secrecy and eventual complete disarmament."

We shall thus, by this first step, have accomplished
more than effective control of atomic power. Oppression by a government is only a secondary cause of
great revolutions. The initial cause is the impotence
of governments, their incapacity to deal with social
and industrial troubles in time. Look where you will
at the present moment, you will find a growing
inability on the part of governments to restore prosperity or to keep pace with the demand for social
reform. The root of the troubles from which men
suffer is not that governments have too much power,
but that they have not enough. In my first talk with
Sir Malcolm Stewart, he said to me that he had
always found the way to social reform barred by two
obstacles. "One cannot," he said, "get people to
apply their minds to social reform so long as they
are looking round the corner for the next war. But
apart from this, effect cannot be given to social reform
without measures which Whitehall and Westminster
are too overburdened with business to devise and to
pass into law."

The three years I spent in Whitehall as a government servant were terrifying. It was often my duty
to attend cabinet meetings and to see major decisions
taken by ministers who had had no time to read the

papers in which the information as to whether such decision should be taken was given. It is not possible for men so overburdened with administrative detail to study the facts and think out the issues to which they are committing the nation. How can a Foreign Secretary who must spend much of his time in cabinet meetings and in Parliament dealing with social and industrial questions in his own country, find time to study facts in Europe, Asia and Africa upon which the issues of peace and war depend? No human being could do it.

For the same reason our Imperial system was in danger of breaking down. Two years ago some Prime Ministers or their deputies met in Downing Street and decided only that they could decide nothing. Their proposal to liquidate the Imperial Conference was met with such general outcry that fresh efforts were made to call another, which met last month. But this temporary effort cannot change the outstanding fact that it is almost impossible for the Prime Ministers of countries like Canada, South Africa, Southern Rhodesia, Australia and New Zealand to find a time when they can all meet the Prime Minister of the United Kingdom round one table. And the difficulty grows as countries like India, Pakistan and Ceylon acquire Dominion status and a right to send their Prime Ministers to the Imperial Conference.

The obvious remedy is for one set of ministers of be made responsible for domestic affairs in each to these countries, while matters which affect them all together, that is to say, the Commonwealth as a whole, are relegated to a government responsible to them all. This solution and no other will give us the control we need of atomic power. For that reason its awful threat to our very existence is a positive godsend. In compelling us to face the ordeal of merging sovereignties in one international sovereignty it is forcing us to remove the great obstacle which bars our return to prosperity, and to open the road to the fullest social reform.

It cannot be done by visionary schemes for including the whole world in one international union. Experienced democracies must first show that it is possible for nations divided by oceans and different languages to merge their sovereignties in an international state under a system which gives to one government responsible to all the charge of interests which are really common to all, such as the issues of peace and war of which the control of atomic power is now an important aspect. All other interests must be left where they now rest, with existing national governments.

If once the world can see such a system is working, nations outside will be anxious to join it, as and when they are able to do so. To include totalitarian states with democracies or politically backward peoples in Asia or Africa which have not yet learned to govern themselves would ensure the failure of such an experiment in advance. It would either collapse in a year or become a despotism, when the last state of the world would be worse than the first.

A century ago my father, waiting for his viva voce,

listened to examiners questioning a candidate who had evidently paid more attention to sport than to learning. An examiner asked him the rather malicious question, "Could you suggest an instance of Providence?" The sportsman instanced the nostrils of a bull-dog which were placed so far back that the dog could breathe while he still held on to the bull's nose. The examiner commended the sportsman, who got his degree. Were I asked that question to-day, the instance I would give would be the release of atomic power at the present juncture of affairs. A shock no less is needed to open men's eyes to the danger of giving criminals power to destroy society, without first giving society the power to control them.

Criminals, like wars, are the product of poverty and all manner of social evils with which our political system as now organized is unable to deal. For physicists, chemists and biologists to release powers of nature which enemies of mankind can turn to wholesale destruction until society has been so constituted as to exercise control over all its parts, is what Shakespeare called "Midsummer Madness."

Our present position was well stated by Sir Stafford Cripps when he said:

"World federation has hitherto been looked upon as a very long-term objective, but the atomic bomb has telescoped history and made it impossible for us to wait long years of acute danger of war, because from the war civilization and mankind cannot survive. We may have a few years yet in which the atomic bomb is not a common weapon in the hands of all major Powers, but they will be pitifully few compared to the immense task that confronts us."

I agree with Lord Russell that a world government is the goal at which we must aim, and must also reach if civilized life is to survive; but I differ when he adds that he does not think the democratic road to world government is practicable. I see no other road to a world government, except by creating a world despotism, which, in my view, would be worse than the total destruction of human life on this earth. The one ray of hope he offers is a world-wide hegemony of the United States. Thoughtful Americans would, I believe, recoil from putting their country in such a position. It is true that in the nineteenth century the United Kingdom did exercise such an hegemony. On the high tide of the industrial revolution we were able to prevent world wars from 1815 to 1914, that is to say until the internal combustion engine had begun to change the whole strategic position. The other democracies came to think that the task of preventing war could be left to the people of these small islands, and even now have failed to realize that we no longer command the human and financial resources required to discharge the cosmic task. The idea that one nation should be held responsible for keeping the peace of the world is based on the assumption that the duty of keeping the peace must be left to sovereign states. It ignores the truth that peace can now be kept only in so far as the duty of keeping it is laid on the people themselves. That is why I believe no system for keeping the peace will be lasting or effective, which has not been approved and accepted by the electorates of all the peoples concerned. The wars of the twentieth century were the opening acts of a world revolution, which sovereign governments have sought, and are still seeking, to evade. Until we establish a system which makes ordinary people realize that the final responsibility for preventing war rests on themselves and not on their national governments, the threat of a third war will hang like a storm-cloud over mankind.

We are often told that in politics as in medicine there are no panaceas: a truism like this covers over and conceals the deeper truth that we cannot solve our political problems unless we establish the rule of law. We had to begin by creating national states to enforce the rule of law within definite frontiers. But institutions fashioned in one age to effect a particular purpose will, if treated as ends in themselves, be a bar to the furtherance of the same purpose in a later and riper age. When national sovereignties have come to be regarded as belonging to that order of nature which cannot be changed, they are fatal to measures for ending the anarchy which must by nature persist between sovereign states. The result is not only to plunge us in wars which may end civilized life, but is no less fatal to the power of sovereign governments to cope with the scarcity of food, clothing and shelter, and the dislocation of industry that war leaves in its train. These sovereign governments are failing to discharge their primary function of providing a better life for the people they rule. We are blind as the fool's heart if we do not see written on the walls of our physical laboratories, that we are weighed in the balances and are found wanting until we extend the rule of law to the whole of this earth.

The atomic pen which traced this warning was held, I believe, by the fingers of God.

AMERICA AS ATLAS

D. W. BROGAN

WHEN I decided to fall back on the old rhetorical device of a classical allusion to provide me with a title, I was naturally tempted to invoke the legend of Prometheus. In a series such as this, in a world consciously or unconsciously obsessed by fear of the new and largely unknown powers usurped by man, emphasis on the Promethean role assumed by the government of the United States is natural. After the destruction in a single blow of Hiroshima, after the news of the radio-active fish of the waters of Bikini, after the acceptance of the fact that new forces have been let loose in the world and that, as an American expert has put it, there may literally be no place to hide, emphasis, even nearly exclusive emphasis, on the present monopoly of atomic power by the United States is natural. It is also wrong, for the present and presumably temporary monopoly of atomic power by the United States is not the main source of American power at the moment and that the United States has a monopoly (which may only be a head start) is important as illustrating the character of American power even more than it is intrinsically important and, if you like, ominous.

So I have chosen the legend of Atlas rather than

the legend of Prometheus, for it is at the moment more important that the United States bears so much of the economic and political burdens of the world than that the United States has the power (should she, i.e. her rulers choose) to impose anything from terrible losses to destruction on the great cities of a possible adversary. If we concentrate our attention merely on this power of destruction, we shall both neglect the other aspects of American power and their relationship to the present American monopoly of the new powers of destruction.

At the present moment, for instance, the chief American weapon in political warfare is not the ownership of the atomic bomb, or the implied threat of its use; it is the economic dependence of a great part of the world, in a sense of the whole world, on the economic power of the United States. If the Western nations find themselves incapable of totally free action, politically or socially, it is because they are dependent on the United States for the freedom of action that comes from having at least the minimum resources of food and raw materials necessary to keep production and the standard of living at the present drab level.

It seems to me, therefore, worthwhile to begin by stressing some truths that I think pretty nearly self-evident and which are yet neglected. And the first of these is that our economic dilemma, our dependence on America, is not in itself profitable to America, is not planned by America, is not entirely the result of the war, or at any rate the result of the last war.

Ever since the end of World War I, all Western Europe in varying degrees has suffered from what we now call a "dollar shortage." At no time since 1919 have we, in Britain, been able to balance our accounts with the United States; nor have the French; nor have the Canadians. Why we escaped the limitations on our independence that we now have to accept was because we lived in a state of peace, uneasy peace, but nevertheless peace in which the wealth of the world was rising and we were sharing absolutely if not relatively in that rise. That American commercial policy in the inter-war years limited the rise in wealth is, I think, true. But as our absolute impoverishment is due to the late war (as is, in the main, the impoverishment of so much of Europe and Asia), the United States is only guilty of that impoverishment to the extent that she is guilty of the coming of the second World War. And that guilt, if America shares it at all, is shared with nearly all the world. America is not responsible for our poverty and has not planned or welcomed or brought about that dependence on the American economy which we most naturally regret and equally naturally, but far less wisely, often resent to the extent of imputing it to America instead of to our own and the world's inability to prevent war.

I have thought it worth while to insist on these platitudes (as they seem to me), just because they do not seem platitudes to other people. The economic *predominance* of the United States is due, in part, to our impoverishment, but the wealth of the United States is not due to that impoverishment. True, the United States escaped comparable impoverishment because of luck but we, too, had our luck; the luck of not being invaded like France and Italy; the luck of having time to make up for sloth and blindness. The Atlantic and Pacific Oceans are merely more obvious examples of geographical luck than the English Channel; they are morally on the same level. We may pity ourselves; we may ask the Americans to pity us; but we should be more than foolish if we both pity ourselves and, however obscurely, think that we are in some sense the victims of American immunity. To wish that the losses of war should fall on others is natural and not wicked from the point of view of this world. It was the wish of the American people in 1939 and the (temporary) achievement of the Russian government in 1939. It was possibly the wish and policy of the British government in 1938. The failure of such a policy may be a matter of regret, but it is not a ground for policy when it *has* failed. The Americans don't owe us anything for our being unlucky and discussions of America's role in the world which tacitly assume that they do, merely blind us to the realities of our own situation.

It is time to turn to the other side of this medal, to the question of how far American economic well-being is due to other forms of luck. It should be obvious, I think, that the United States did not

profit out of being a belligerent. We may have been
forced to sell some American assets at a bad price;
we may have suffered competitive losses in Asia and
Latin America; but how trifling were these American
gains compared with the waste of American resources
in Europe, all over the Pacific, in the steel sunk at
sea, the petroleum products wasted in air and naval
war, the three hundred thousand young men lost
from the ranks of producers forever! You can't put
the burden of war on posterity. You must pay it at
the time and America has paid her share of war losses
at the time. True, the unused resources, human and
material, of 1939 were profitably used by 1942, but
full employment and full utilization of resources
(including irreplaceable resources like oil) at the
cost of a war like the last one is a bad bargain—or so
the world still thinks and wisely thinks.

But there remains one form of luck which the
United States has and which accounts, in part, for
her present Atlantean position. America has great
natural sources of wealth. Without her coal and iron,
oil and natural gas, she would not be in her present
dominating position. It would be foolish to ignore
that, just as it would be foolish to ignore the degree
to which the Soviet Union before the war owed a
good deal to the luck of having oil and gold and
platinum or the degree to which the economic
system of Britain in the nineteenth century owed its
leading role to coal.

Just as there is a temptation to attibute American
economic predominance to the luck of comparative

immunity from the losses of war, there is the corresponding temptation to attribute it, for the most of the remaining part, to the mere natural resources of the United States. And that temptation is succumbed to both for naïve human reasons of resentment and jealousy and, I fear, for ideological reasons, too. For in societies whose climate of opinion is increasingly collectivist, the makers of that climate are naturally perplexed by the fact that in the least collectivist of countries the mere production of material wealth has gone farthest, that the doom of non-collectivist economies is postponed again by the dependence of collectivist or semi-collectivist societies on the great heretical state and that dependence inevitably limits the freedom of action of states moving, so they believe, with the tide of time to a more abundant life. For that tide moves slowly indeed and, briskly swimming against the current, the United States seems to be doing rather better than those societies that have, so they think, the tide with them. It is again natural and again unfortunate that this state of affairs should produce resentment; what is deplorable is that it should produce blindness and it does produce blindness.

It is deplorable because we are involved with the Americans in a relationship which only day-dreamers believe we can escape. And that relationship can be more or less good for us according to the skill with which we (and of course the Americans) adjust ourselves to it. We can trust the Americans to make their own mistakes; we should devote most of our attention to minimizing our own, at what cost to *amour propre* it is not for me to say.

We must refuse to imitate the Greeks who unable to deny the fact of Roman power, refused to understand it. So I think it will be profitable to consider, however, briefly, the nature of American power, in all its relevant aspects, including the presnt monopoly of atomic power.

And that involves some consideration of the nature of American society for even if we do not go as far as Lord Russell in welcoming an American hegemony, we cannot escape the fact of American preponderance. It will pay us to assess it with as much coolness as we can command and, if we cannot command complete objectivity, with at any rate an open admission of bias. And I share with Lord Russell a deep conviction that nearly all that we treasure in our own inheritance is far safer in American hands than in the hands of the only alternative society capable of organizing the world.

II

There is a preliminary difficulty in assessing the fitness of the American people to give a lead to the world or their worthiness to own, even temporarily, the monopoly of atomic energy. Because of the general character of the American social and political system, i.e. its lack of a single organizing principle, it must be hard to assess. Against any particular attribute that may be given it by the observer, another observer can set a contrary attribute and back up his description with good examples drawn from American sources.

If we, for example, follow the not very wise example set by some American publicists and spokesmen and make of the United States the great examplar of "free enterprise," we run at once into difficulties. The more simple-minded American businessman assumes that there is such a self-contained system, that American life exemplifies it and that it is so evident a good and so undeniable a phenomenon that it hardly needs defining or defending. The United States is the product of free enterprise; the United States has the highest standard of living in the world; therefore free enterprise exists, is justified and need not be further described. There are visible and irritating signs of this mentality in America and among Americans outside America, for example in Germany and Japan. Yet it is easy enough to demonstrate that free enterprise does not exist in this simple sense in America, has perhaps never existed and, at any rate, has certainly not existed for a long time.

The American business man may think that, in the not very recent past, he or his predecessors could do as they liked with their own. But he is wrong. For high protective tariffs (which in the mass the businessman supports and has supported for three generations), prevent the buyer doing what he likes with his own dollar. So with regulation of railroad rates or the penalizing, by the courts, of secondary boycotts by trade unions, or the land policy of the federal government, or shipping subsidies; all are derogations from the presumed pure ideal of maximizing the free choice of the producer or worker. So, too, are the anti-trust laws whose desperate and perhaps futile effort to keep the free enterprise system from ending up in a group of giant monopolies, at least testifies to the complexity of the problem—and the vagueness of the term.

Yet such is the fascination of the phrase and such the temptation to vanity as well as greed with which its repeated use exposes the user, that many otherwise responsible businessmen think there is something abnormal, possibly downright wrong in a government monopoly of the production of atomic power. Even if only as a token of the dedication of the United States to the mystical principle of free enterprise, business should be allowed some finger in the pie. That the control of the production of atomic power is a problem not to be solved by repeating formulas; that the whole international bargaining position of the United States is called in question by leaving it open, even as a possibility, that atomic power may be manufactured for private profit are matters of no great moment or so it would appear. Still more striking is the ability to forget that the very existence of that power is due exclusively to government enterprise. No corporation, however great, could have commanded the resources necessary to create Manhattan Project and the other centres of production. No private corporation could have seen any justification for the dissipation of its resources to destroy Hiroshima. Surely there could be no greater proof of the hynoptic effect of the vague concept than that one of the two leading contenders for the Presidency in 1948 toyed with the idea of *some* participation of private business in the production of atomic energy! (It is also worth noting that the candidate in question was, despite all the prophets, defeated.)

On the other hand, it should be noted that private enterprise did play and does play a great role in the whole complicated scheme of atomic energy production in America. As Professor Oliphant has pointed out, most of the basic research in this field was begun in Britain and even if most of the final scientific work was done in America, it was largely, done by European scientists. What America contributed (apart from immense material resources) was that very American thing described by the very American neologism, "know-how." And that know-how came very largely from the laboratories and workshops and workshop practice of great, competitive, privately controlled businesses. In this combination of business and government (with the first choice and final decision in the hands of the government), lies far more of the secret of American wealth and power than is to be found in any simple and exclusive formula.

Yet such formulas have their numbing power. In Germany for example, it is by no means certain that the minimum resources for recovery by allowing for the curative forces of nature, i.e. by free enterprise, exist at the moment. A patient may need a massive blood transfusion or a major operation even if the physician would prefer to trust to the milder ways of nature. Whatever professional prejudice or suspicion he may entertain, he must call in the surgeon. Whether this be the case in Germany or not, it is probable that the diagnosis has been delayed disastrously long while the professional squabble went on. And some of that bias can be seen elsewhere, too.

That we have much to learn from American methods in our production is, I think, undoubted. But as Mr. Harrod, Professor Allen and others have pointed out, a blind imitation of American methods, with no regard to the limiting conditions of our resources in men and capital might be quite disastrous. Yet many Americans think of the export of their industrial methods with the same simple faith in their universal and easy applicability that was felt by the good Liberal in Britain last century when it was a question of exporting the British parliamentary system.

If we assume that American business overestimates its role and its sacrosanct character we shall be right. But we should also note that it overestimates its power—and that we tend to do so too. For a great deal of the suspicion of American policy that is so great a force in the world to-day has at its roots the belief that all American policy, at home or abroad, is dictated in all except minor and generally deceptive detail by an entity called "business" whose only god is profit. If this be so, then behind American policy and the instruments of policy lies the greed of business and we must find economic motives of this type for even apparently generous moves, for the outpouring of many billions of dollars in relief, for the promise of more under the Marshall Plan. "What is in it for them?" is assumed to be the proper approach and the "them" is assumed to be this identifiable group, the businessmen. If this were so, if the world were at present being led and is perhaps to be ruled by a nation of shopkeepers (in the pejorative sense of the term), the high price of security under American dominance might seem very high even if not too high to pay.

But it is not so and never has been so. For there is no such entity as business in the sense of a group of interests collaborating together in pursuit of common interests. At times it is perhaps a pity that there is no such united group as exists in the imagination of polemists. For business, if united, would be ruled by Big Business and its rule might, if only on the grounds of enlightened self-interest, have been wiser and more far-seeing than was the policy of the United States made by the diverse pressure groups that imposed high tariffs, barred immigration and, in general, diminished both the wealth of the United States and the stability of the world between the two wars. We must accept the fact that business is not the exclusive ruler of the United States and that business is not a united interest.

In a sense, we flatter the public morality of the

American businessman when we see him dreaming of foreign worlds to conquer. The American economy is under no such temptation or rather pressure to export as our economy has been for over a century past. Exports are marginal to the American economy and there has long been an open contrast between the aims of American foreign policy and the immediate interests of American business. Latin-America has never been as important to Wall Street as to the State Department and Japan was a far more important customer to the United States than was China right down to Pearl Harbour. It is to be the slave of a theory to see in the Marshall Plan a mere device of American business faced with a loss of markets; if it were only that it might not exist and would certainly be on a much smaller scale. True there are sections of the American economy which have an acute interest in exports and in making the American taxpayer replace the once solvent European importer. Cotton, tobacco, films are examples of these interests and, if they had their way, Marshall aid would be earmarked in the first place for taking care of surpluses. Not only do these interests not dominate either the American economy or the administration of the Marshall Plan, but the administrators of that plan have to fight at least equally hard—and not always equally successfully— to secure exports for the countries in need of help, for the American buyer dislikes very much being outbid by a European buyer with American funds provided by the American taxpayer. As long as the

American economy is on a boom basis, there is next
to no pressure (to put it mildly) to export, still less
to encourage free exports.

But if there is a slump? Then it might be wise to
replace by government spending the declining pur-
chasing power of the American consumer. But why
must it be done by spending on exports, i.e. un-
requited exports? Why not internal exports; why
not rebuild the South instead of Europe, create
customers in the underprivileged classes of the
United States? There may be answers to this which
economists can provide, but I know of none which
is likely to satisfy the American voter or the American
Congressman who has to vote the money. It would
be foolish, in such circumstances, to create fresh
problems by cutting Marshall aid but Congress
might be foolish. And, indeed, I find it dismally
significant that people should think that an American
recession would help us more than it hurts us or
should mix-up the fact that American inflation hurts
us with the fiction that we should gain more on the
swings of the terms of trade than we should lose
in the decline in demand for our exports, a demand
whose present inadequacy even in boom times is the
chief source of our economic troubles.

No, the American Atlas is not bearing his burden
because of the cash profits he can expect from those
he saves from immediate economic catastrophe. He
has a profit in mind; it would be idle to deny that.
No nation however rich and however generous is
gratuitously charitable on this scale. But what the

Atlas expects for his pains is a world in which peace, the mere peace of the absence of hostilities, the better peace of co-operation and confidence can be secured or hoped for. What the American government wants and the American people is willing to pay for is something of the security that (it was fondly hoped) had been won in Europe and in Asia in 1945.

That all the peoples of the world wanted peace then and want it now may be taken for granted. But not all peoples have the opportunity of demonstrating their violent desire for peace, for the relaxation of the tensions of war, such as were open to the American people in 1945. It was reflected in the speed with which demobilization was rushed (to the great weakening of the political weight of the United States); it was reflected in the speed with which economic weapons in the hands of the government were thrown or snatched away, to the very serious loss of Europe as well as of the United States. It is the greatest tribute to the negative success of Russian policy and Russian manners that, three years later, the American people have accepted peace-time conscription, continued high taxation, the Marshall Plan, and the underwriting of the independence of Western Europe. If we accept (as I think we must), that the present objects of American policy are political and that the limitation of Russian control of the remaining independent nations is the chosen means to the main end, the survival of the independence of the United States, at a less cost than would be imposed by having to try to live a free nation in

a Russified world, American policy becomes intel-
ligible—and economical. Our doubts will centre
round American political ability to carry out the
policy, unless, of course, we think the aims of that
policy wrong or unimportant or not worth the
probable price in economic sacrifice.

But if we do think the aim worth a high price,
partly to be paid by us, partly to be paid by the
United States; if we dismiss, as at any rate in-
adequate, the simple theory that sees in American
policy, merely cold war as the extension of business,
we are still left with the problem of the political
responsibility and maturity of the American government and people. Are they for instance lucky children
who have to have the greatest accumulation of old
and new weapons? Are they simply the profiteers of
the world's present economic distress? Can they be
expected, even if their policy is sound, to implement
it? Even if we stop far short of Lord Russell's thesis,
we must want to know what confidence we can
repose on American policy and promises. History is
an imperfect guide and as far as mere precedent
goes, not a very encouraging one. It would be
foolish to forget 1919 and the American withdrawal into isolationism. If that is to occur again,
the sooner we know it the better. The results of such
a withdrawal would be very unpleasant indeed but if
it is to come we had better get used to the unpleasant
prospect:

> 'Tis true there's better booze than brine
> But he that drowns must drink it.

Nor even if American policy stays fixed will we always find it agreeable in detail. It is a common ground of fear or resentment of the Marshall Plan that it involves interference with national sovereignty, an objection often voiced most vehemently by persons whose care, at other times, for national sovereignty, their own or that of other peoples, is not noticeably vocal. If by national sovereignty we mean the absolute right of each nation to do as it likes with its own, that still remains. The question is has a nation an absolute right to do as it likes with another nation's own? The question needs no answering. The United States has, in the past, made many outright gifts, but the European recovery programme is based not on a policy of gifts but of what we can call, by English analogy, "grants in aid." And that involves conditions. To expect otherwise is to continue to live in a dream land. But what is not unreasonable is to fear that American conditions may be too much affected by *a priori* bias in favour of "free enterprise"—just as our reactions to such a bias may be equally dogmatic and unrealistic. We may be too insistent on equipping ourselves with all the luxuries that appeal to our planners and Americans may be too impressed by the need of political and economic rationalization of the old and complicated European society that they are attempting to shore up.

But there is one doubt that can only be resolved in practice, a doubt that the American political system is adequate for the tempo of the age. In one

K

way this is reassuring. No governmental system is less well designed for aggressive war or for the preparation for aggressive war. The division of powers between President and Congress and between the houses of Congress; the limitations of the written constitution; the fixity of elections, the elaborate machinery of controls; the lavish provision of instruments of publicity; these are very serious impediments to the activities of a Hitler or a Tojo should we suppose that a Hitler or a Tojo is likely to be in power or, straining our imagination a little further, *is* in power. Things are not often done in a corner in America   at least in peace time. And as the publicity that is somesafeguard against a sudden blow or the temptations of preventive war, has some unfortunate aspects, we should be thankful for the kind of reassurance that we can get from it. For it *has* its drawbacks. American policy is hammered out with a great deal of noise and recrimination. It is open to the mischief-maker and the fearful to pick what alarming words he wants from the roaring winds of American controversy. But the general trend of American policy is not aggressive nor is the national temper. No neighbours of America now live in fear of forcible intervention; Panama can demand the withdrawal of American air bases without being afraid that the United States will refuse to pay attention to the formal sovereignty of a state she created. You can stage a revolution in Bogota with grave inconvenience to the visiting Secretary of State with no fear of reprisal.

American policy is not only unaggressive; it is often hesitant and uncertain. As far as it is based on economic aid for Western Europe, it is threatened by the division of powers in the American system. For the policy made by the executive may be mutilated by the legislature. And both are deeply responsive to pressure groups of all kinds; to Jews in New York who wish to promote the interests of Zion; to Poles in Detroit who wish the American government to abandon a "realistic acceptance of facts" behind the Iron Curtain. It is open to less passionate pressure, say from shipping groups who want in effect to limit the dollar-earning power of the dollar-starved countries. It is possible, at times, to despair of the possibility of American leadership being equal to American power and consequent responsibilities. It is difficult, indeed, to see in this mixed, tumultuous, divided society the centre of a premeditated conspiracy against the peace and well-being of the world, except in so far as the occasional incoherence of and frequent changes in American policy (in detail at least) add to the uncertainties and so to the dangers of our fear-tormented condition.

But it was, we should remember, that fearfully divided nation that rallied after the first terrible disaster of Pearl Harbour and, inside four years created the greatest navy, the greatest air force and one of the two greatest armies in the world. It was this society that provided the matrix for the manufacture of the atomic bomb—and this divided government that made the bomb and kept the secret. It is also this society and government that twice after being one of the main makers of victory, has demanded no reparations, no rectifications of frontiers (though the American borders have oddities enough).

It is a society that insists that its chief behave like a civilian even when he is a soldier and that prefers to turn its ploughshares into swords, rather than to have its sword ready in advance. It is for this reason that America is underwriting Europe, that she may not have to live armed to keep her goods in peace— with the ruinous consequences that Mr. Harrod has outlined. She has—and knows she has—an interest in prosperity and stability. Only in a world that is stable and prosperous can America avoid being forced to give away a good part of what she makes by her own toil or see the nations descend further into misery with all its power to promote further disaster. It is not the fault, in the main, of America, that she is a new magnetic mountain. No doubt a wiser tariff and fiscal policy would lessen the strain—on us and on her. But we must work out our salvation, no doubt with American help but mainly by our own efforts. And surely Atlas may be permitted a little peevishness at times as he listens to the barrage of criticism with which he is assailed by the very peoples defended from ruin by his assuming of what is a heavy burden, great as is his strength?

But Atlas is also Prometheus. It is perhaps a pity that there is any Prometheus. Even if we put the possible economic gains of atomic fission a good deal

higher than Mr. Harrod does and the risks even
lower than Professor Blackett does, we may still
think that the price in fear is too high. But Atlas is
also Prometheus and can we doubt that the world
would be still more nervous if his secret were
exclusively in the hands of another state, with no
publicly divided councils and with no known control
of its policies and actions? It is the reasonable hope of
all reasonable Americans that their role, as Atlas,
may in not too long a time, make, in perspective,
their role as Prometheus far less important than it
seems now. If and when the time comes that their
secret is not only no longer a secret, but their means
of exploiting it no secret either, we may hope that
the burden will then be less exclusively Atlas's, that
we shall be able to share it. But until that day, if such
new powers there must be, it is at any rate something
that they are in the hands of a people that in Lincoln's
words strives "to bind up the nation's wounds" and,
as I believe, basically seek no more than "to achieve
and cherish a just and lasting peace, among ourselves, and with all nations."

For Product Safety Concerns and Information please contact our EU
representative GPSR@taylorandfrancis.com
Taylor & Francis Verlag GmbH, Kaufingerstraße 24, 80331 München, Germany